BLACKS IN HISPANIC LITERATURE

Kennikat Press
National University Publications
Literary Criticism Series

General Editor
John E. Becker
Fairleigh Dickinson University

Miriam DeCosta
EDITOR

BLACKS IN
HISPANIC LITERATURE

CRITICAL ESSAYS

National University Publications
KENNIKAT PRESS   //   1977
Port Washington, N. Y.   //   London

Manufactured in the United States of America

Published by
Kennikat Press Corp.
Port Washington, N. Y./London

Library of Congress Cataloging in Publication Data
Main entry under title:

Blacks in Hispanic literature.

(Literary criticism series) (National university publications)
    Bibliography: p.
    Includes index.
    1. Spanish literature—History and criticism—Addresses, essays, lectures. 2. Spanish American literature—History and criticism—Addresses, essays, lectures. 3. Blacks in literature—Addresses, essays, lectures. I. DeCosta, Miriam.
PQ6046.B56B6   860'.9'352   76-45192
ISBN 0-8046-9140-1

The strong men . . . coming on
The strong men gittin' stronger.
Strong men . . . .
Stronger . . . .

there stood a secret manhood tough and tall
that circumstance and crackers could not kill
                                    —my husband, "A"

Neither chants nor wails nor mournings fill
the emptied place obscure the memory nor
heal the heart, what
compensates for
eyes . . .
        gentled at the corners so
        from loving
                                        —Daddy

Remember the face of the warrior
Whose name knows a multiple doom
Before he is born to follow the eye
To the shapes remembered where the spirit moves
On to the darknesses the eye caresses
In us and into us and ours.
                                    —my son, Tarik

Contents

Preface

Critical appraisals of Afro-Hispanic literature were undertaken in the Thirties with the pioneer studies of Carter G. Woodson, Valaurez B. Spratlin and John F. Matheus. The works of these prominent Black scholars have been of particular significance to a group of younger Hispanists who were trained in universities where Spanish literature was studied, analyzed and interpreted within the context of Euro-American scholarship, but whose own research interests and efforts turned to the Black (both as author and fictional persona) in Hispanic literature.

There have been many studies of Afro-American and of Francophone literature, as scholars have attempted to define, classify and categorize the new Black Aesthetic, creating terms and concepts which define and describe "Blackness" or "Negritude" by developing critical perspectives that emanate from and are a part of a particular socio-historic experience. Although there have been several individual studies of Afro-Hispanic literature, *Blacks in Hispanic Literature* is the first collection of critical essays by a group of distinguished Black scholars.

Eight of the articles included in this volume have been published before, and it is significant that six of these articles have appeared in two journals, the *Journal of Negro History* and the *CLA Journal.* These two pioneer publications, under the editorship of Carter G. Woodson and Therman B. O'Daniel respectively, have been important touchstones of twentieth-century Black thought. The other six articles were written especially for this collection, and the editor is extremely grateful to these promising young scholars for the efforts that have gone into their research and documentation.

This work represents a collective response to several ideological, academic and pragmatic imperatives. It is designed to acquaint the English-speaking scholar with a body of literature with which he may be unfamiliar, as well as to serve as a basis of comparison and contrast with other African and neo-African literatures to determine if there is a Black Aesthetic which transcends linguistic and cultural barriers. Further, it is intended to stimulate students of Hispanic literature to undertake individual and collective research (analysis and interpretation of texts, translation of Hispanic works into English, preparation of materials for the classroom), which is so vital at this moment in history. Finally, it is designed to encourage university professors and administrators to incorporate Afro-Hispanic studies into the traditional Spanish curriculum and to foster independent undergraduate study, graduate research and collective faculty research in this academic area.

Blacks in Hispanic Literature was made possible by a research grant from the Faculty Research Program in the Social Sciences, Humanities and Education at Howard University. The editor is particularly appreciative of the support and encouragement of her research efforts by Dr. Theodora R. Boyd, former Chairman of the Department of Romance Languages and Dr. Andrew Billingsley, the former Vice President of Academic Affairs. The commitment of the faculty and the administration of Howard University to quality education for Black men and women has created an exciting and stimulating academic environment in which the contributions of African peoples can be systematically analyzed, evaluated and appreciated.

BLACKS IN HISPANIC LITERATURE

MIRIAM DeCOSTA

Introduction

Afro-Hispanic literature flowered in the Thirties, when the turn-of-the-century cult of the Negro erupted full bloom into *negrismo, Négritude* and the Harlem Renaissance. Negrist scholars, including anthropologists, folklorists, musicologists and literary critics, viewed the Black Movement primarily as an exotic offshoot of Post-Modernism, Indigenism, Surrealism and other such "isms" which titillated the twentieth-century imagination, sated as it was on heavy draughts of Freudian psychology, Bergsonian philosophy and Baudelarian fin-de-siècle decadence. According to these "scholars," negrismo was not a genuine literary movement and Black writers did not constitute a legitimate school; in their view, negrismo was a passing literary fancy and the negro was of minimal significance in the Latin American white/indian/black racial mélange. This view was soundly rejected by scholars such as Carter G. Woodson, John Hope Franklin, Alain Locke, John F. Matheus and others, who underscored African contributions to New World history, language, literature, music, art and social institutions. These early Afro-American scholars played a significant part in the discovery, appraisal and dissemination of materials (both historical and literary texts) which documented Black contributions to European and American society.

   One of the major objectives of Black Criticism is to structure a critical framework for the analysis of literature, a framework which takes into account the unique historical (or experiential) situation, the cultural context and the ideological/philosophic milieu out of which Afro-Hispanic literature has emerged. There is an implicit relationship between literature and history, especially in the minds of scholars who insistently have viewed their race's creative works within the larger social context, eschewing the European, ivory-towered "l'art pour l'art" aesthetic and interpreting Poetry as instrument of Truth and Liberation.

The relationship between literature and history can be analyzed both deductively and inductively. On the one hand, the "historical" method of literary criticism views literary creation deterministically as the end result of a particular set of historical imperatives. According to this interpretation, the exploitation of the Cuban masses by capitalist and imperialist foreign interests created the socio-political climate which, in turn, produced the protest poetry of an Arozarena or of a Guillén. Conversely, Montejo's *Biografía de un cimarrón* or Manzano's *Autobiografía* are considered more significant as historical documents which describe nineteenth-century Cuban slave life than as literary works. Black Criticism, on the other hand, interprets literature as more than passive poeticized history — the imaginative end product of socio-political forces; instead, it adumbrates the power of Poetry to create Image (an *individual* intuition of reality that transcends *res*) and Myth (product of the *collective* imagination). According to this view, literature shapes and directs man's perception of himself and of his society. Wright's Bigger Thomas or Ellison's Invisible Man or even Superfly/Shaft/Sweetback (mere coincidence that the initial *s* evokes the familiar four-letter expletive?) recreate themselves in Black society. The fictional persona thus projects (in words or on screen) a preexistent "type" which in turn reproduces itself in real life as people emulate the model. History produces Literature, but, conversely, Literature creates History.

The historical interaction of Africa and Spain in the past millennium can be divided into three rather distinct periods: (1) African ascendancy from 711 to 1200, imagistically evoked by an eleventh-century Moorish poet, "A Black man was swimming in a pool where the waters did not hide the pebbles on the bottom," (2) African enslavement from 1500 to the late 1800s, a time of "Half opened veins and eyelids / And empty daybreaks," and (3) Spanish colonialism (and U.S. domination thereafter), when, as Pedroso tells his Black brother, "For your enjoyment the rich make of you a game ... they manufacture Negroes of straw for exportation." Although much has been made (by the Other) of the integration, syncretization and assimilation of the African and Spanish cultures, it is more realistic to view the relationship as one of confrontation, when two radically divergent cultures were traumatically juxtaposed in the experiences of war, slavery and colonization. The Moorish invasion of the Peninsula, for example, produced a seven-hundred-year state of siege between two peoples whose differences were both racial and religious. The confrontation between Islam, propagated by the sword, and Christianity, imposed by atrocious "Holy Wars" and genocidal *autos da fe,* was violent;

this violence was recorded in historical documents such as the *Rayham al-alhab*, the *Kitab al-iqtifa*, and the *Kamil al-Tawarij*, as well as in literary works such as the *Cantar de Mio Cid* and the *Cántigas* of Alfonso the Wise. The African occupation of Spain, as well as the enslavement of Blacks and the colonization of the New World, must be understood and analyzed if one is to interpret, for example, the relationship between Third World politics and twentieth-century Caribbean literature.

Black scholars like Fanon, Franklin and Knight have used the instruments of modern science — psychiatry, sociology, anthropology and sociolinguistics — in reinterpreting African/American history, and in assessing the impact that existence in an alien society has had upon the development of Black institutions. These scientific tools have given the Black scholar an *objective* base for judging and evaluating history; equally important, however, in shaping attitudes and judgments is the scholar's personal and his race's collective *subjective* experience as Blacks in a white society. This objective/subjective dichotomy must be synthesized by the literary critic who is trained in the methods and techniques of Euro-American criticism but who finds that he also needs a different framework and new criteria for analyzing and conveying intuitive (and perhaps, to the Western mind, iconoclastic) perceptions of "reality," of "forms of things unknown." The Black critic must use the craft of Western scholarship to his own end, but he must control this Frankenstein monster (fabricated of bits and pieces of Platonic/Aristotelian aesthetics, Medieval/Renaissance world views, Hegelian/Marxist methodology and existentialist/structuralist criticism) by a thorough understanding of Black history and literature, a sensitive appreciation (built on fact and not romantic fiction) of the race's contributions, and an analytical approach which can be utilized in a collective effort to create new concepts, new definitions and new critical structures.

The concepts of Addison Gayle, Don L. Lee, Carolyn Fowler (Gerald), Stephen Henderson, George Kent and others can serve as points of departure to the Black critic of Afro-Hispanic literature and culture — points of departure, beginnings, provocative thoughts, a conceptual base for the examination of all neo-African literature. Black American writing/ criticism (for the two are conjoined in the Poet/Prophet/Preceptist) has destroyed, as Gayle explains in his September 1974 article in *Black World*, some cherished "American" postulates: that literature can "convert" the racist; that protest literature will change the white's Black-as-Monster image into Black-as-Prince; that Black writing is a vehicle of social mobility and "acceptance"; that the major theme (the only theme) of Black literature is the gratuitous suffering of the castrated Black man, deballed on the American cross, and all other such mythic "truisms." Such views have been reduced to smoldering ashes, from which has risen, phoenix-like, the Black Aesthetic, affirming and positing a new view of literature. Perhaps not *a* new view, because the theories, concepts and conclusions are as varied, diverse and mutable as are the colors of Black people. Some preceptists would reject Western aesthetics completely; others would apply Western methodology — textual analysis based on thematic, linguistic or structural studies of content and form (*fondo y forma*) — to Black literature.

However, undergirding the diversity of approach are intimations of unanimity, suggestions of shared experience and intuitions of collective ideology. Primary is the shared experience of the apocalyptic holocaust and the "deliberate desecration and smashing of idols, the turning inside-out of symbols." It is the destruction of past beliefs (those of the Other) which *determined* our ethos, our aesthetic, our ontogeny and even our cosmogony. Then the rebirth, re-creation, conversion and fiery baptism. American poet become Black poet. *Annie Allen* transcended in *Riot*. And, finally, the search for roots, the "odyssey back into [the] cultural heritage," to an ancestral African home where non-Western images, symbols and metaphors create a different reality: Shango, high life, Shaka, *tambor,* Songhay, Askia Issehak, *Nam* (powerful juju-imposing rule), Nubia and the "Children of the Sun." Images of the time B.C. (before God became white) and B.P. (before Prospero conquered the Land). Writers engaged "in a black-white war over the control of image," because, as Fowler explains, "to manipulate an image is to control a peoplehood." Black writers (Poets/Rebels) constructing a man-centered anthropomorphic world where human values (read Black humanism) take precedence over the dollar, the computer and the bomb.

Afro-Hispanic literature creates and projects its own Image and Myth, Image and Myth which in Camagüey (Cuba), Esmeraldas (Ecuador) and Loiza Aldea (Puerto Rico) sprout unalloyed from ancestral and animistic roots. Africa survives and is metamorphosed as Shango becomes *Changó;* the mythic Bantu *Quimbungo* is converted into the Ecuadorian jungle creature, the *Tunda;* the prototypal Tarik prefigures "el Rey Miguel," ruler of a Black Venezuelan kingdom; *kingombo* in the Ki-mbundu language becomes Puerto Rican *quingombo*/American "gumbo"; and the African drum evolves into the Cuban *bongó, gongo* and *tumba.* How different are the images, symbols, metaphors, archetypes (and the multiple smells, sounds, tastes) of Black American literature and culture: Crispus Attucks, the dozens, Simple, spiritual/blues, "scent of pine needles/ And the smell of red clay after rain," the KKK, Ma Rainey, Thunderbird and Ripple, Louie's trombone. One wonders whether the two life-literatures (Afro-Anglo and Afro-Hispanic) run along parallel trajectories and continuums or whether there is an axis, a point of convergence, where the two cultures meet. Common to both is their Africanity, a heritage variously expressed in songrhythm, wordrhythm, liferhythm; the Middle Passage and exile in an alien land; the experience of outsideness, invisibility, peripheral being in a non-Black majority culture (existence under the unblinking gaze of the Other) and, above all, the strengths — endurance, resiliency, affirmation/protest and the ability to cope. This is not to suggest that the differences (Hispanic vis-à-vis Anglo) are not equally salient: the differences are geographic (coconut plantation/cottonfield), historic (*quilombo*/slave revolt), political (*miguelismo*/Black power), cultural (Cuban *comparsa*/ Mississippi Baptist revival), linguistic (*guineo*/Black dialect), and psychological (*mulatismo*/"passing"). However, it is through the systematic comparison and contrast of African and diasporic cultures that the literary historian can understand and appreciate the Black man's unique contributions to the Western world.

SYLVIA WYNTER

The Eye of the Other: Images of the Black in Spanish Literature

In his book on the Jewish Question, Sartre points out the tragic imperative of the Jew in Western civilization, to constantly question himself and confront "that phantom person, unknown and familiar, ungraspable and yet near, that person that haunts him, and that is no other than himself as he is seen by the Other".[1] Both in his literary work and in his philosophic thought, Sartre distinguishes three modes of Being: Being-in-Itself, Being-for-Itself, and Being-for-the Other. The first, Being-in-Itself, is the external world. The second, Being-for-Itself, is human consciousness. The third mode of Being is the being that each man has for other men. At the beginning of an acquaintance, each sees the other as a mere Being-in-Itself, as a natural phenomenon. It is through his look, his gaze, that the Other reveals himself as a Being-for-Himself.

Sartre is here basing himself on and extending the doctrine of Hegel which postulates that our self-consciousness exists only for another person. Self-consciousness is, finally, recognition on the part of the Other. Each is an object for the Other, the Other who looks and judges; each needs to obtain the recognition of his Being from the Other. The Other is the mediator between me and myself.

Hegel argued that self-consciousness is real only to the extent that it recognizes its echo in another person. Sartre develops this further, arguing that if we exist for others we exist by and through their look. The look of the Other not only reveals to me that I am an Object for him, but also that the Other is a Subject.

Extract from a book in progress, *The Eye of the Other: Essays on the Black as Fictional "Other" in the Literature of Spain and Latin America.*

For the eye is not only a physiological organ which looks at me; it is the other person as consciousness. Thus, the look of the Other includes all classes of judgments and valuations. To be seen by the Other means to apprehend oneself as an unknown object of unforeseen configurations. The fact of being seen changes me into a person defenseless before a liberty that is not my liberty. On being seen by other persons we are slaves. Looking at other persons we are Masters.

In the novel *The Invisible Man*, Ralph Ellison makes this Eye of the Other the central problematic of his work. The narrator begins his story:

I am an invisible man. . . . The invisibility to which I refer occurs because of a peculiar disposition of the eyes of those with whom I come in contact. A matter of the construction of their inner eye, those eyes with which they look through physical eyes upon reality.

To explore certain basic aspects of the black in Spanish literature, it is necessary to view the black in the context of the "inner eye," the eye with which seventeenth-century Christian Catholic Imperial Spain looked through its physical eye upon the reality of the black Other. Even more important for this exploration is the theory of Pierre Macherey, in his book dealing with the concept of literary production, in which he develops the argument that any writer, in setting out to write a play, poem or novel, is faced with preexistent conventions, devices, and formulae, within the limits of which, or perhaps more precisely *with* which, as his given means of *production*, he must produce his work from the raw materials of his historical experience, his given historical *situation*.[2]

Let us look quickly at the key facts of this historical situation. In the mid-fifteenth century, Europe — Portugal, to be exact — discovered Africa, and discovered her as, above all else, a source of slaves, of labor power to work on the latifundia — the large estates recaptured from the Moors, who, in 1492, after some eight centuries, had finally been driven from the Iberian Peninsula. The need of the Iberian latifundia for labor power was to determine the increasingly widespread presence of the black on the Peninsula. The black was, therefore, to be incorporated into Western civilization, its fact and fiction, through the institution of the latifundia.

But in the mid-fifteenth century, the economic motive was still subordinate to the societal whole, at least symbolically, and the black presence was defined and categorized not in economic but in religious terms. As early as 1551, Antao Goncalves and Nuno Tristao, both of the retinue of the Portuguese Prince Henry, the Navigator, returned from Africa with the first load of black captives. The prince was pleased at this lucrative "trade" and the chronicler who relates these "bold exploits" piously adds "that although their bodies were placed in subjection the fact was of small importance compared with the eternal freedom of their soul."[3]

The ideology by which the Christian nations of Spain and Portugal would at once pose and resolve the problem of the black as slave and the black as Christian subject was paradoxical. Indeed, the justification for enslaving not only blacks from Africa but Indians from the recently discovered New World, a justification couched in terms of exchange by which the "native" gave his material labor power in exchange for his spiritual freedom, would be central to the debate which later raged, among whose main protagonists were Las Casas and Sepulveda. Other theologians both supported and rejected this rationalization; one, in particular, reasoned from the tenets of Natural Law that there was nothing in the Law of Christ which stated that "the liberty of the soul must be paid for by the servitude of the body."[4]

But the ideology which provided the rationalization won out, as the material bases — the extension of the latifundia, the discovery of the New World, the decimation of the Indians following their widespread enslavement, the replacement of Indians by black slaves — increasingly dictated its imperatives. In the seventeenth century, the ideology would not be altogether racial; indeed, its tenets were still partly religious, and it was a logical extension of the practice of both Mohammedans and Christians (as well as of Africans) of keeping prisoners captured in war as slaves. The paradox of the situation in the seventeenth century was, however, that just as the slavery of Western man began to disappear from Europe, it expanded in the Iberian Peninsula and in the New World as the black was enslaved. What has been referred to as the dialectic of freedom and unfreedom had begun.[5]

After the establishment of the slave trade by the Portuguese, the dominant fact of black existence in Spain and Portugal was his existence not as a black, but as a *slave*. A Spanish Capuchin missionary, Antonio de Teruel, pointed out in a narrative that he wrote of his mission to the Congo in the seventeenth century that the Congolese

do not wish to be called blacks, but swarthy. Only slaves are called blacks. And so, as far as they are concerned, it is the same thing to say black as to say slave.[6]

They were all "naturally" black, they warned; they were *not* all "naturally" slaves. But the warning went unheeded. Through the institution of the latifundium in the Iberian Peninsula, and the plantation in the New World, the black entered the Western architecture of signs conjoined as fact and fiction — black slave. He was black (*negro*) because he was naturally a slave (*esclavo*); he was a slave (*esclavo*) because he was naturally black (*negro*). To be a Negro was to be a slave.

Literary images of the black predated the Portuguese discovery of Africa in the fifteenth century. These images responded to the reality of an earlier and established black presence. This presence was related to a reality contrary to that created by the Portuguese African slave trade. The earlier black presence was related to the Arab conquest of Spain in the eighth century and the assertion of the Mohammedan faith, rule and culture on the Peninsula.

The Mohammedan religion expanded with missionary impetus throughout northwest Africa and into the Iberian Peninsula, as the Moors, including many pure blacks, enlarged their empire. In her valuable article on the portrayal of blacks in a Spanish medieval manuscript, Miriam DeCosta shows that the actual historical reality of black Moors appears both in the illuminations and the text of the thirteenth-century *Cántigas*.[7] The black Moor is portrayed as the opposed term to the Christian religious metaphor. Like the other Moors, he is cast in the dread role of infidel, invader and defiler of Christian altars. The Moor, "black as pitch," was not only the opposed religion; his color was the opposite of "white," symbol of Christianity. It is important to note two important aspects of this relation, this symbolic structure. As the writer points out, the black Moor was not "denigrated (or feared as the case may be) because of his color, but because of his religion." Also, the relation of the black Moor, symbolically, to the Devil was a relation which sprang from a reality in which the Mohammedan was the dominant power. The "black as devil" concept sprang from an impulse which, as Lemuel Johnson points out, is similar to the twentieth-century Black Muslim definition of the dominant Westerner as "white devil."[8] The use of symbols, in myth, religion, legend, literature has powerful consequences.

In literature, the topos by which the prevailing reality is criticized by turning its structure of symbols upside down is known as *adynaton*. This topos was traced and studied in early Western literature by Curtius. Indeed, Macherey's more modern insistence on the only partial "autonomy" of literary forms, on the fact that literary devices are never "neutral" but weighted with former accretions of significances, was prefigured by the patient reconstructions of Curtius in his book on *European Literature and the Latin Middle Ages*, even though Macherey was to put this method of investigation to somewhat different uses. Curtius, in his illuminating chapter "The World Upside Down," writes:

The frame of the antique adynaton serves both as censure of the times and denunciation of the times. Out of stringing together impossibilia grows a topos: "the world upside down."

The dominance of Islam in Spain was, for the Spanish Christians, the "world upside down." In Christian symbolic terms, the black Moor became the "god upside down," assimilated to the Being whose presence indicates the absence of an implicitly white Christ/God — the Devil. This play-paradox between the white Sacrament and the black skin of the Negro would later become a central literary device.

In analyzing the *Cántigas*, Miss DeCosta underscores the counter-missionary aspect of thirteenth-century Christianity. Such is the power of the Virgin Mary that she is able to rescue a black Moor from the Devil, and to convert him to Christianity. Thus, the power of Christianity is exalted by its capacity to *convert* its opposite (in terms of color) to its own faith, to its own white/Christian identity. But the opposition is essentially one between Mohammedanism and Christianity. While in the *Cántigas* the image of the Moor and the black are interchangeable, the myth of Prester John, which was pervasive in the Peninsula, saw the black legendary figure as constituting a third, and separate, figure. The original legend had located Prester John in Asia, but the legend itself was one of many exotic Western myths.

Henri Baudet, in his book *Paradise on Earth: Some Thoughts on European Images of Non-European Man*, points out that Europe, originally an outpost of Asia, was a "classic invasion area open to all manner of migrations and expansion movements sweeping in from the east." It was only with the Greeks, who took to the sea, that Europe developed a consciousness distinguishing Europe from Asia, the West from the East, the European from the non-European." This consciousness, which structured the inner eye with which Europe would look through its physical eyes upon the reality of the Others, was further developed by the stream of invasions and threats of invasions from the East which marked the history of Europe until well after the Renaissance. This "semi-permanent state of siege, of attack and counter-attack" helped to create the "defensive mentality" with which Europe responded to the "recurrent threat of an Asiatic tidal wave that would engulf the entire continent." The Mohammedan invasion of the Iberian Peninsula was part of this general movement.

Baudet goes on to point out that the Greeks shaped the European spirit by a dual opposition/orientation towards Asia — much as the "Third World" today shapes its own consciousness by a dual opposition/orientation towards Europe — and this led to a paradoxical process of hostility/inclination, rejection/reabsorption towards the people of the outside world. This dualism was apparent in the myths and fantasies of the Greeks, who imagined archetypal peoples at the four quarters of a great inhabited land mass. They created the monster stereotype, a race of non-European monstrous people, dog-headed men with eyes in their chests. Ethiopia, which figured in these early myths, was, according to the Greeks, a land of "remote" peoples who became either objects of a Golden Age dream (i.e., Noble Savages) or threatening monsters projected by the undergrowth of the European imagination. But the Christians changed the classical image of Ethiopia (land of the Ethiopian Eunuch) to the archetype of the Christian convert. Finally, the memory of the Ethiopian Eunuch (the potential convert) came to be assimilated to the legend of Prester John; and it is this legend which functioned as a device that would be central to literature, especially to the pastoral. For it is clear that the Ethiopia of Prester John is the imagined antecedent of the *locus amoenus*, the pleasant spot, which alludes to and contradicts the real world by that which it selects, and that which it eliminates. What is eliminated in the legend of Prester John is robbery, poverty, sin, death, and the contradiction between the Christian faith, which denies the world, and the Christian State, whose raison d'etre is power in the world. What was retained was saintliness, charity, hospitality, abundance, rejuvenation and the marvelous. The retention and the elimination delineated the features of a pastoral "Golden Age." Prester John, to the hard-pressed Christian world facing the real power of the Mohammedans, became a dream of Christian power, a projection of power by the relatively powerless.

In the situation of a locked and equal struggle between two variants (Christianity and Mohammedanism) of a religious truth, a third, an outsider, is imagined by one side; he is an outsider who validates the truth of the Christian side in the imagination and whose imaginary reality helps to structure the Christian's conviction of his own truth. The Christians' creation of the legend of Prester John, and Lope de Vega's creation of the Mohammedan black Prince Antiobo, who converts to Christianity and fights the Mohammedans, respond to the same impulse. The inner eye that imagined Prester John, and the inner eye of pre-Lope Iberian writers who created changing variants of the black figure in response to changing situations, would themselves set up a process of creation which would help to structure the eye of later writers. The images of the black in Hispano-European literature, although related to the stereotypes of the esclavo in real life, respond also to a more complex and, at times, separate process. Baudet puts this well:

The relationships, separated but indivisible, are always apparent in the European consciousness. One is in the realm of political life in its broadest sense, in the atmosphere of . . . concrete relations with concrete non-European countries. . . . The other relationship has reigned in the minds of men. Its domain is that of the imagination, of all sorts of images of non-Western peoples and worlds, which have flourished in our culture — images derived not from observation, experience and perceptible reality, but from a psychological urge.

The image of the black in Hispanic literature responds to the second relationship; yet, at the same time, it mediates between the second and the first; its projection of the imagined relationship is always related to the "real" relationship, and — except when, as "bad" literature, it is reduced to ideology and, as such, only reflects the myth — it at once embodies the myth and is critical of it.

If, in religious metaphor, the image of the Black Moor Devil in the *Cántigas* is opposed to the Christian Prester John of the legend, in social terms, in medieval literature, the images of the black varied from king to slave. The reality of the *prieto* was not yet reduced to esclavo, and indeed it would be only with the expansion of the capitalist mode of production that this reduction would be made. One aspect of the medieval portrayal of the black, whether as king or as slave, is the idea of the black as a marginal man, an outsider. In the mid-twelfth-century *Auto de los Reyes Magos*, King Baltasar is not described as black or Moorish, specifically. Howard Jason describes him as such, most likely bearing in mind the traditional development of medieval Christian drama based on the feast of the Epiphany and the dramatic *Officium Stellae*.[9]

Karl Young, in his study of the drama of the medieval church, points out that a description of the Magi, most likely dating from the twelfth century, describes the first king as *senex, canus;* the second as *rubicundus;* and the third, Baltasar, as *fuscus* (i.e., "dark").[10] The tradition of the *fuscus* Moorish king was in the literary tradition which developed with medieval church drama. Young shows that the tradition of the three kings was intended to prove that the Christ child was king of all the earth, of all peoples. If we assume that Baltasar, in the Spanish twelfth-century *Auto de los Reyes Magos*, responds to this tradition, then his implicit delineation as Black-Moor is seen as the extreme form of the heathen-sage, whose science must see itself superseded, yet realized, in the Child-King of the Christians. For in the *Auto*, King Baltasar is in a sense the most skeptical and the "most scientific" in a play in which doubt exists in dialectic with affirmation.

The skepticism of the black king links this image with that of the *negro* in one of the stories of *El Conde Lucanor* written by Don Juan Manuel in the first half of the fourteenth century. In this story, a king was deceived by three men who told him they could weave a cloth of such virtue that only legitimate sons could see the fabric. When the duped king rode naked through the streets, his pretentious subjects marveled over his fine "robe," until

a Negro who looked after the King's horse and *who had nothing to lose,* came to the King and told him: "Your majesty, it doesn't matter to me whether people think me the son of that father that I say I am or the son of another; therefore, I can tell you this — either I am blind, or you are naked."

The black, who tended horses, had no possessions and, therefore, no need to worry about his lineage, since preoccupation with lineage was linked to the possession of goods, which could be inherited. He is, therefore, the perfect example of what Sartre defines as the "contingent man," the marginal man, who can be truly revolutionary because he is outside of the prevailing social structure and its concomitant ideology.

The black sees the truth because he is in an existential situation where, to borrow an Althusserian formulation, he has no need to *over see* the truth.[11] His factual existence makes it possible for him to negate the prevailing consciousness, to demystify one variant of the dominant ideology. The *negro* is the outsider, the "lump" in the social structure. The black as *skeptical* heathen Magus/King, and the black as *skeptical* marginal outsider (the second even more distinctively so) are the literary devices by which the writer — who exists in a dual relation to the official reality of his society (i.e., a part of it, yet marginal to it) — poses the *ideology* of his society as a problematic.

Juan Manuel's story can very well be seen as the exemplification in art of the critical comment that Althusser goes on to make:

What art makes us *see*, and therefore gives to us . . . is the *ideology* from which it is born, in which it bathes, and from which it detaches itself as art, and to which it alludes. . . .

Baltasar questions the "science" of the revealed truth, although he finally accepts it; the *negro* contests the ideology by which the others sustain a reality in which they all have a stake. The Eye of the Other, of each, conspires in the collective fiction. The Eye of the Other, which is literature, reflects and contests the fiction. In the story, it is the black's eye which functions as the literary Eye of the Other. Thus, the legendary Prester John and the black existentially skeptical outsider emerged as literary formulae with which post-medieval Iberian literature would structure the image of the black.

With the introduction of the Portuguese slave trade in the fifteenth century, the image of the black in literature, responding to the new reality, alternated around the axis of king/slave. The image of Prester John as a powerful king fades as the reality of Ethiopia, itself relatively powerless in technological, warlike terms, dislodged the myth. The slave/king axis of the post-medieval black image was first projected in Portuguese literature. Here, the black appeared in the farcical/satirical mode; that is, he was portrayed as a comic type in the low style of literature which dealt with the rustic.

By the mid-sixteenth century, the black-as-slave was a pervasive presence on the Iberian Peninsula. There are references to the Negro presence in the fifteenth-century *Cancionero geral* by García de Resende (c. 1476–1536), and in these presentations of the black, certain constants are already structured. One of these constants is language, the stage language, or *negroide*, which was put into the mouth of the black. In a poem by Fernam de Silveyra, written before 1485, the black appears as the King of Sierra Leone. Although a king, his language is negroide, a fabrication which draws on an already established linguistic stage convention. According to Frida Weber de Kurlat, this idiomatic deformation of Spanish "is deeply engrained in the medieval secular tradition that utilized the mixture of languages, primarily Latin and the vernacular language, for satiric or comic purposes. . . ."[12]

This identification of the Negro through his use of a deformed Castilian Spanish was primary in the development of the stage Negro. This linguistic stereotype in literature was to parallel the factual stereotype of the black, even though the literary usage would carry positive elements foreign to the real stereotype. The kind of "sambo" language which defined the stage black referred to a characteristic peculiar to the black-as-slave — his use of a language, Spanish, which he learned only through the oral process and which he picked up without any formal instruction and transformed, accordingly, to his own linguistic emphases. In the factual stereotype, the black's version of Spanish was seen as evidence of an incapacity, an inability to grasp language — language seen ethnocentrically as Western language.

Stage negroide presents the black not only as comic, but also as uneducated. When Antiobo, the hero of the second half of *El negro del mejor amo,* is portrayed as a prince who speaks perfect Castilian, his speech is a sure sign that he is the exemplary black. Speaking of the Negro in the Caribbean, Fanon notes that, "he will be proportionately whiter — that is, he will come closer to being a real human being — in direct ratio to his mastery of the French language."[13] From the beginning, the comic Negro becomes, according to Johnson, "negatively decorative and as slightly obscene as a Gargoyle." In his valuable book on the black as metaphor in Western literature, Johnson picks out as significant in the Hispanic context the use of the stage *negro* linguistic convention, and compares this with the absence, in English literature, of a Negro voice. Othello, for example, does not speak in an "identifiable Negro English." This caricatured Negro voice, Johnson argues, "allows for several levels of parody — the visible physiognomical oddity, the quality of song, and the precariously dislocated Spanish in which the voice sings." As we shall show, negroide is used for two effects: one, comic caricature, the other lyric. As with later Afro-Antillian poetry, the dialectic of lyricism/caricature refuses the reduction to the one element or the other. The lyric elements contest the caricatured elements and vice versa.

It must not be forgotten that the black presence was assimilated to the strong current of *lo popular* which was central to Hispanic literature. It was out of this tradition that Luis de Góngora, perhaps Spain's greatest poet, whose poetry achieves a superb fusion of *lo popular* and *lo culto*, wrote poems about blacks in which the caricature element is negated by the lyric intention. In one of Góngora's *letrillas*, "En la Fiesta del Santísimo Sacramento," two black women, Juana and Clara, speak. The poem is balanced between caricature and lyricism. But the truth of the situation, the black girl constituting in her person the symbol that negates the white symbolic purity of the metaphor of the Sacrament, imposes itself. The figurative language of the poem, its black/white antithesis, responds to the lyrical despair of Clara (note the name), who, in rejecting the color black as the anti-symbol of the Sacrament, rejects herself. The tone is playful; the intention is not.

The actual desire of black slaves, the dream which negates their real situation, fuses with that "promesse de bonheur" which is the imperative of all art. The caricature aspects of negroide are contested and redeemed by authentic lyricism, in which reality and its transposition in literature demands the use of negroide, not as a cultural cosmetic but as an artistic imperative. For blacks to voice their imperative of human freedom, from their actual existential situation, a literary voice has to be found for their real voice. This real voice is redeemed of its caricature elements and is transfigured.

The constant of a stereotyped language was soon matched by the established constant of the *negra* as metaphor of unbridled licentiousness and sex. Cervantes, in his account of the development of Golden Age theatre in Spain, wrote that in the time of Lope de Rueda

The plays were dialogues like ecologues between two or three shepherds and a shepherdess; [these plays] were pepped up and enlivened with two short pieces about a Negress, or a rogue, or a fool, or a Biscayan....

Lope de Rueda uses his *negra* type to satirize the most deeply rooted obsession of Spanish society — its obsession with noble lineage. The noble lineage/honour/*limpieza de sangre* axis was central to sixteenth- and seventeenth-century Spain. These constituted the social passion of the upwardly mobile. However, in these plays the black slave, who can have no ancestry to speak of — who is not self-aware, as was the *negro* in Juan Manuel's story — shares in the mania, the persistent obsession of the society, and reveals its ridiculous aspect. The comic eye of Rueda distances itself from the obsessive ideology of the time, the myth by which all Spaniards shared in the collective fiction that noble birth or pure Christian birth were the norms on which human society was built.

Another constant of the black image is the Black-as-Eunuch. Indeed, the black as sexual monster, the bad nigger, is one side of the dialectic; the black as Eunuch, or Uncle Tom, is the other. In Cervantes's exemplary novel, *El Celoso Extremeño,* the servant/slave Luis is physically a eunuch. In the portrayal of Luis, one of the constants of the black type also appears — the black's love of music. Cervantes uses this stereotype for the purpose of art. He makes Luis's relation to music central to his story. An old man, having married a very young wife, puts his eunuch slave to guard the only entrance to the house. The suitor suborns Luis with music, playing the guitar and promising to teach the Negro certain songs. In this way the young man gains entrance to the house. Cervantes had observed a real fact — the black's adherence to dance and music — and used it for artistic rather than caricature effect.

The affinity of blacks for music and dance was noted by an early chronicler, who pointed out that in Seville

Blacks were treated with great kindness, since the time of King Henry the Third, who allowed them to congregate for their dances and celebrations on holidays, *so that they would be more amenable to work and would better tolerate their captivity.*[14]

The same chronicler narrates how the blacks organized into *cofradías;* they took full part in the Corpus and other religious processions and customs. The fact that a *popular* religion like Iberian Catholic Christianity existed made possible the transculturation. Dance and song were transplanted; the exiled gods took up their new place behind the masks of the saints. African dance, called by one anthropologist "the liturgical technique of the body" and "one of the typically African means of sustaining a dialogue with the gods," metamorphosed the gods.

The stereotype of the dancing/singing minstrel *over-saw* an important truth: the black transplanted the dance because it was a central part of the oral/ritual structure of his religious world. As time passed, and Africa and his origin became remote, the world of this symbolic universe deserted him, this universe which had defined his former being. Fragments, powerful ones, remained. But the black, like Caliban, was now exiled from his structure of meaning. Dance became disjointed from religion. But it existed as collective art, as non-alienated physical "labor," the adynaton, the world-upside-down of his daily reality of forced labor. The former universe as metaphor fell apart; the fragments remained, obsessive by their very disjointedness. The eye of the writer saw these fragments and used them either for art, as in Cervantes's story, or as the caricatured stereotype of ideology and the stock characters of inferior literature.

NOTES

1. Jean Paul Sartre, *Réflexions sur la question jüive* (Paris, 1946), p. 101.
2. Pierre Macherey, *Pour une théorie de la production littéraire* (Paris, 1966).
3. Raymond Sayers, *The Negro in Brazilian Literature* (New York, 1956), p. 15. The reference is to Azurara, the fifteenth-century chronicler of the Conquest of Guinea.
4. Bartholomé de Albornoz, in *Obras escogidas*, ed. F. Carlos Sainz del Robles (Madrid, 1946), Vol. I, p. 84.
5. Joel Kovel, *White Racism: A Psychohistory* (New York, 1971), p.15.
6. Padre Antonio de Teruel, *Descripción narrativa de la misión seráfica de los capuchinos, y sus progresos en el Reyno de Congo, 1663-1664,* Ms. 3533, Biblioteca Nacional, Madrid. (In the process of being edited for publication.)
7. Miriam DeCosta, "The Portrayal of Blacks in a Spanish Medieval Manuscript," *Negro History Bulletin,* 37 (1974), pp. 193-196.
8. Lemuel Johnson, *The Devil, the Gargoyle and the Buffoon: The Negro as Metaphor in Western Literature* (Port Washington, N.Y., 1971), p. 175.
9. Howard M. Jason, "The Negro in Spanish Literature to the End of the Siglo de Oro," *CLA Journal,* IX (December, 1965).
10. Karl Young, *The Drama of the Medieval Church* (Oxford, 1951), Vol. II, p. 31. Young takes these descriptions from the twelfth-century *Collectanea et Flores* of Pseudo Beda.
11. Louis Althusser, *Lenin and Philosophy and Other Essays* (London), p. 203.
12. Frida Weber de Kurlat, "El tipo del negro en el teatro de Lope de Vega: tradición y creación," *Actas del Segundo Congreso Internacional de Hispanistas,* Instituto Español de la Universidad de Nijmega (Holland, 1967).
13. Frantz Fanon, *Black Skins White Masks,* trans. Charles Markham (New York, 1967), p. 18.
14. Ortiz de Zúñiza, *Anales ecclesiásticos y seculares de la ciudad de Sevilla,* Lib. XII, 1474, p. 374.

MARTHA COBB

Afro-Arabs, Blackamoors and Blacks: An Inquiry into Race Concepts Through Spanish Literature

For a long time history and literature, dominated by the orientation and attitudes of European scholarship, have conspired to hide the impact that Africa once had on the development of culture and civilization. To deny this past is to ignore a significant part of both African and European history, to be unaware of the constantly changing human relationships of the past that have evolved into attitudes and concepts about Black people in the modern world.

From ancient times Spain served as a bridge between Europe and an Eastern world whose cultural crossroad was Africa. Situated at the extreme southeast of the European continent, the Iberian Peninsula very nearly touches Africa in the Straits of Gibraltar. Bearing out this reality, we can still see in the Alpera Caves in the southeast of Spain a treasury of stylized drawings of African origin that represent men and women and animals. These sophisticated drawings of figures in movement are focused on the central themes of hunting and the dance. On the other hand, in the Altamira Caves in the north of Spain are found the simpler drawings of animals on the walls that are European in origin. It is interesting to note that scholars now admit that it is the representations of African origin on the walls of the southeastern Alpera Caves which are the first cultural document of European life rather than those that lack human figures found in the northern Altamira Caves.[1]

Successive waves of human beings entered Spain, but the indigenous population was composed of the Iberians, a dark people considered to be of African origin, a fact that the Caves of Alpera sustain. The people who

From *Black World*, 21 (February, 1972), pp. 32-40. Reprinted by permission of the author and *Black World*.

are the concern of this study, however, are the Moors, who came into Spain in 711 A.D., defeating the Visigoths and initiating a struggle between Christianity and Islam that lasted until 1492 with the triumph of the Catholic monarchs, Ferdinand and Isabella. During this time, a second Moorish invasion, under the African general Yusuf in the eleventh century, extended Moslem rule for approximately one hundred years from the Senegal River in West Africa to the Ebro River in northern Spain.

Some modern writers like to call the Moorish invaders Arabs, but this term is incorrect. What actually happened, as the writings of the time can testify, is that a minority of Arabs (themselves an interracial group) left their homeland to push the Moslem religion westward and to gain new lands. They converted the people in their path to Islam — the Mohammedan religion. Their converts were Africans: East and North Africans, Egyptians, men from the Sudan — the "land of the Blacks," others from the Zenaga Berbers who gave their name to Senegal, and a mixture of many more, most of whom were so dark they were called blackamoors by Europeans.

During the Moorish domination, Spaniards themselves used the term *Moors,* which indicates more accurately that the invaders crossed into Spain from the continent of Africa and that it was Mohammedan Africans rather than Arabs who defeated Spain. Yusuf's warriors, who were drawn from both West and North Africa, were called Almoravids, which may give a linguistic clue to the origin of the term Moor. As we shall see, literature expresses the profound influence of these historical facts on Spanish culture and, as a result, through Spain, on the culture of other parts of the European continent.

We must bear in mind that during this epoch of Islamic invasions and Moorish power in Spain, Black civilizations flourished in West Africa and extended their influence northward. The empires of Ghana, Mali, and Songhay advanced to successive heights of civilization in Africa during the "dark ages" of medieval Europe. Between the Africans of these empires and the Islamic Arabs there flourished a commercial, religious and cultural interchange which included matrimony between Arab and African and the development of education in African universities, such as that of Timbuctu, which attracted scholars from all parts of the Moslem world.

Thus, the Moslems who dominated Spain were not a homogeneous people. On the contrary, they were Arabs united with African peoples — on an equal basis if they converted to Islam, otherwise enslaved if they were conquered, as many white Europeans were enslaved during the same epoch for similar reasons. Modern studies included in many American textbooks have eliminated references to Africans, using the word Arab as if Arabs were a pure (unmixed) race, or perhaps a white race. Neither is the case.

One of the most distinguished Afro-Arabs, honored and well known in the Eastern world, was Antar. His full name was Antar ιbn Shaddad al'Absi, and he lived before the Islamic era and the invasion of Spain. The son of a Black woman from the African continent and a Berber Arab, Antar was renowned as a warrior, poet, and the ideal representative of a chivalric code which, according to the legends that followed his death, he formulated. His *Mo'allaqua,* or "Praise Song," which hung in the Mosque at Mecca, is considered a masterpiece, one of the seven golden odes of the Arab world. Typical of the poets of those feudal times, Antar related his conquests in war and love, as the following lines illustrate:

> Before the spearmen's deadly thrust she tried to rouse my fears
> As if I were defenseless and unarmed against their spears.
> I answered her, "Now surely death is no more than a pool,
> And some day I must drain the cup dipped in its waters cool.
> So fare thee well, care for thy young, and tell thyself once more
> That I'm a man who's either making love or making war.
> Privation many nights and days I easily can bear,
> Knowing that in the end I'll gain of noble food my share."

It is also interesting to discover that Antar took pride in his Black pigmentation. Thus:

> In blackness there is great virtue, if you will but observe its beauty . . .
> Black ambergris has the purest fragrance . . .

After his death in 615 A.D., the tradition of Antar spread because his celebrated career and writings were perpetuated in song and story through the efforts of a group of storytellers and poets, his disciples, who called themselves Antaristas. In the course of time, Antar legend and poetry flourished in the Eastern world, like later tales of chivalry that were written in Spain and France, or the King Arthur legends of England. It was this Antarista tradition, brought to the Iberian Peninsula by the Moors, that formed the base of many European romances of chivalry and later influenced the development of the codes of chivalry in medieval Europe. According to one scholar, "the Antarah was the most important of the oriental originals on which some of our own Christian romances of the Middle Ages were founded."[2] Joseph Freiherr von Hammer-Purgstall writes: "This is the work, and not, as is generally supposed, the *Thousand and One Nights,* which is the source of the stories which fill the tents and cottages in Arabia and Egypt." In this same context he adds that "the very spirit and substance of chivalry migrated with the Arabians from the East, through Spain to Europe."

A contemporary Spanish scholar and critic notes in his book on Arab literature that the Antar tradition has a parallel in the cycle of stories based on the French hero Roland, and that this needs to be investigated further to verify the former's influence on the later epic poem, *Song of Roland*.[3]

Following Antar, other Moors, who were recognized as Black men, were to contribute to medieval scholarship and literature in Europe. For example, there were Abu Dulama Ibn Al Djaun, poet in the court at Baghdad in the eighth century, and Ziriab (Zirvab), better known to his contemporaries as the "Black Nightingale," who arrived in 822 in Spain, where he resided at the court in Cordoba. Others were Ibn Darray, poet; Abu Bakr, warrior and poet; Ben Said Al-Magribi, geographer, traveler, scholar, poet, a writer of note. Serious inquiry into the lives and works of any of these men suggests the possibility of significant contributions that can be made in the scholarly field.

Another historical figure who attests the confluence of the Arab, African and Spanish worlds in the early Middle Ages was Tariq. He was an African warrior who converted to Islam when the Arabs moved across North Africa, and was made a general to support Arab troops with his African army. When Tariq discovered the possibilities of invasion, he crossed over into Spain twice in 711, the second time in command of an army of seven thousand Africans that defeated the Gothic king of Spain, Rodrigo. He was later joined by Musa ben Nusayr, leading Arab troops to reinforce that victory. Together they pushed further into Spain, but the initial conquest belongs to Tariq and his Africans. Mons Calpe, where Tariq had built an encampment and left a garrison to secure his communication with Africa, was renamed Gebel Tariq by his troops in his honor, a name which meant Hill of Tariq. It was this name, Gebel Tariq, which later was transformed by the Spanish into Gibraltar.

On the European continent, literature, folklore and fine arts bear out the historical reality. The Spanish language also reflects a cultural amalgam that existed nearly eight hundred years. Semanticists might take note that the word for blackberry still in use in present-day Spain is *mora,* a feminine noun which originally meant "Moorish woman," and that the adjective for "dark-complexioned," which now means "brunette," is *moreno* (that is, "Moorish").

At this point an attitudinal change with reference to Africa and Africans must be indicated. On the one hand, both in antiquity and especially during the Middle Ages, the image of Africa and Africans was generally positive, largely because of their victories in war. In Spanish literature, the African in the person of the Moor is usually of the ruling or upper class. He is frequently characterized as a wealthy person, or a learned person, to whom Spaniards often went for counsel. Often he is pictured as greedy for wealth and power, but in any case to be respected and more than likely admired, even when he was the enemy. On the other hand, the sixteenth century marked a turning point in this image. The Moors were expelled from Spain after 1492. Christianity triumphed in Europe at last. The Moors, falling back on African soil after their defeat and rout from Spain, were a major factor in the sacking and breakdown of West African empires and civilization. For Europe the way was open for the age of discovery and exploration, initiated by Spain and Portugal, that was to result in the colonization and enslavement of Africa and the opening up of the Americas. As a result, Africans (and those of African descent) came more and more to be depicted as primitives, as savages, as slaves. African humanity was denied. In Western thought and literature, Africa became a caricature for barbarism and backwardness, incapable of contributing to the ongoing evolution of world civilizations.

Stemming from these two concepts, and using the sixteenth century as the dividing line, the significance of Africa in Hispanic culture becomes evident. It is this awareness that will serve to clear away the old myths, stereotypes, and misinformation that have pursued Black men into the 1900s.

Literature and the arts in Spain, as well as in other European countries prior to the sixteenth century, substantiate the view of Africans in elevated positions and Africa as a land that evoked both respect and curiosity. Statues of Black kings and the painting of Black Madonnas can still be seen in European churches. The Moor, noble and authoritative figure, has literary counterparts of which Shakespeare's Othello and the Moors of *Titus Andronicus* are major examples. References to Ethiopians and their land as the land of the Blacks and symbol of learning and wealth, the legend and search for Prester John — mythical figure whom medieval Europe, fighting Islam, idealized as the image of Black Christianity in Africa — the symbol of Black Saint Maurice in Germany, are as indicative of the African image in Western consciousness at one point in history as the slave, flooding the markets of Seville and Lisbon, was to become during the 1500s.

A primary source for Spanish writers on Moorish themes is the work entitled *Guerras civiles de Granada,* by Ginés Pérez de Hita. It describes the frontier wars between Moor and Christian that took place on Spanish soil. Dramatists and poets used this book as a source for the colorful Moorish romances and "frontier" stories that became popular in the sixteenth and seventeenth centuries as Spain looked back to her past. One chapter tells of the exploits of a Black named Captain Farax, whose furious fighting made him a hero in the region around Lorca. When at last forced to retreat, he burned the fields around him and in other ways attacked Christians, who fell in great numbers or were made slaves. In retaliation, the Christians tried to burn him alive, but according to the accounts, Black Captain Farax escaped and is said to have fled to Africa and planned other assaults from there. A sixteenth-century playwright, Diego Jiménez de Enciso, in one of his plays modeled a character whom he called Cañerí on this personality, the Black warrior Farax. Other Spanish writers, especially those of the sixteenth and seventeenth centuries, were to use similar episodes for the elaboration of the popular Moorish romances of the era.

Margaret Sampson, in her study of *El Caballero Cifar,*[4] notes that in this prose romance of chivalry dating back to the thirteenth century, Africa is often referred to either geographically or mythically. In addition, the work includes didactic tales and adventure stories which confirm the authoritative position of the Moor in the society of the time.

Much the same can be said for the fourteenth-century tales written by Don Juan Manuel in his masterpiece, the *Libro del Conde Lucanor.* The author utilizes the framework of a storyteller — in this case a counselor named Patronio — who tells moral tales, usually with Moorish protagonists, to illustrate solutions to problems that his master, the Count Lucanor, presents to him. The stories spin on, many of them having their base in tales brought into Spain with the Moorish invasion.

Advancing to the sixteenth century, a different kind of Black personality marks Spanish literature. Moorish leaders and warriors had been routed and expelled. Those who were left were of a lower class and called *moriscos* rather than *moros.* They were poor agricultural laborers needed to work in the fields of Andalusia; they were often peddlers and vagrants who lived by their wits. A triumphant Spanish nobility learned to look down on this dark-skinned people. Furthermore, slaves from Africa were being imported into Spain in increasing numbers. Cities like Seville and Granada now became accustomed to associating Blackness with the inferior slave.

Juan Latino stands out as an unusual representative of this new kind of Black. In 1528 he was brought from Africa (possibly Guinea) to Spain as a slave. Growing up in slavery, he adopted Christianity and learned Latin and Greek from the books of his master's son, eventually becoming the boy's tutor. He graduated from the University of Granada with honors in 1557 and was appointed a professor in the same university. He was so outstanding in Latin that he renounced his slave name to call himself Juan Latino. He was received with acclamation and great respect by the Spanish people throughout a long life that spanned Spain's Golden Age. Both Cervantes and Lope de Vega referred to him or used incidents from his life in their works.

For the most part Juan Latino expressed in his written works a personality that was essentially Spanish in nature. He wrote like a white Spaniard, with no central theme that concerned itself with his African origins nor with the conditions of slavery that he not only must have witnessed but must himself have been subjected to. His marriage to a white Spanish woman, noted and referred to by writers of his time, served to enhance his position. His major literary work was the *Austriad*, with verses erudite in language and academic in style, revealing a patriotic commitment to Spain. Written in Latin, this work by the ex-slave Juan Latino celebrates the Spanish victory at the Battle of Lepanto.

The success of Juan Latino was achieved despite the fact that he was African. The price exacted was that he convert to Christianity, cut loose from his African origins, and adopt the Spanish way of life. By Spanish standards, therefore, he was judged a worthy individual. Thus the balance had tipped against Africa and in favor of Europe. The erudite Ethiopians, fierce Moorish warriors, Black kings, knights and saints, the mysterious Prester John — all who had set standards of culture and chivalry on their own terms — were disappearing from Western consciousness. Juan Latino was himself symbolic of the new age: he was brought into Spain as a slave and he learned to read and master the Latin language through the indulgence of his owners.

For a while the Moor was to linger on in Spanish literature through the popular Moorish romances of the sixteenth and seventeenth centuries that were the themes of such poets and dramatists as Lope de Vega, Luis de Góngora, Francisco de Quevedo, Lope de Rueda and others. Their writing, as in the case of Quevedo, often expressed a duality in concept. His "Boda de negros," for example, exaggerates and burlesques the Blackness of a wedding party, the gestures and manners of the participants, to the point of making fun of them, ridiculing their Blackness. On the other hand, in his "La hora de todos," he expresses compassion for Black slaves in their unfortunate condition. Góngora also demonstrates a dual point of view: he uses the speech patterns and jargon of sixteenth-century Blacks in creating images of their lower-class lifestyle in some of his poetry; in other poetry he goes back to the traditions of medieval Spain in retelling stories of interracial romance between African and Spaniard and recreating the splendor of the chivalric code upheld by noble Moor and Christian alike.

However, the effect of the Renaissance and the age of discovery and exploration in Europe were irreversible in literature. A new era opened up after 1492 in which men of African origin suffered the final collapse of their culture and the indignities of chattel enslavement which stripped them of their rights as human beings. The African of the medieval world was rejected for a different image that must satisfy the economic needs that the new age demanded. Literature would do no less than reflect these changes.

The African — whether called Moor, Ethiopian or Black — gradually disappeared from Spanish peninsular culture. Neither art nor literature took serious note of him. Royalty occasionally made him a court pet. Slaves were sometimes elevated to positions of trust in Spanish households or artists' workshops. Even more significantly, in terms of New World history, they often served as right-hand men, guides, and explorers to Spanish conquerors as they advanced through forest, jungle, and Indian territory in both South and North America. Estevanico is just one example of this breed of slave upon whom Spaniards in America depended. Sometimes references were made to the Moorish past, but more often sixteenth- and seventeenth-century literature portrayed its Black element as buffoons or rascals. Spain was too occupied with setting up a slave trade for extracting wealth from her colonies to perceive the African as anything more than a sub-human species to be exploited.

To continue to trace the literary presence of Africa in Hispanic culture, interested scholars must proceed to the Americas. Spanish American culture reveals that the African way of life found expression in folklore, in the syncretism of African religious practices and Catholic rituals, in music and dance, and in language, all of which were to flower ultimately in the expressive Black poetry of the Caribbean in the early 1920s. An examination of this culture must be the subject of another paper.

Meanwhile, a study of the concepts that mark the distance traveled from medieval Blackamoor to present-day Blacks offers a valuable tool in understanding and defining the African heritage of African peoples in the twentieth century, wherever they are located. The dimensions of research in this field should open up to scholars and educators channels for more study and dissemination of knowledge.

NOTES

1. For recent references to the prehistoric presence of Africans (*iberos*, described as "una raza de hombres bajos y morenos" or "de origen africano") see José and Manuela Cirre, *España y los españoles* (New York: Holt, Rinehart and Winston, 1970), pp. 3-4; Francisco Ugarte, *España y su civilización* (New York: The Odyssey Press, 1952), p. 13. For further investigation into race concepts that refute the "Aryan" theory and Euro-

pean definitions of "Negro" see W. E. B. DuBois, *The Negro* (New York: Henry Holt and Co., 1915), pp. 9-29; and Carter G. Woodson, *The African Background Outlined* (Washington, D.C.: The Associated Press, 1936).
2. Janheinz Jahn, *Neo-African Literature: A History of Black Writing,* tr. from German (Grove Press, N. Y., 1968). (Quotation from Wilfred Scawn Blunt, British orientalist.)
3. Juan Vernet, *Literatura Arabe,* Editorial Labor, S.A., Barcelona, 2nd ed., 1968.
4. Margaret Sampson, "Africa in Medieval Spanish Literature: Its Appearance in *El Caballero Cifar,"* *Negro History Bulletin,* December, 1969.

HOWARD M. JASON

The Negro in Spanish Literature to the End of the Siglo de Oro

"The Negro in Spanish Literature" has interested a number of investigators in recent years. Some of the latest studies include an article by Dr. Juan R. Castellano of Duke University on "El negro esclavo en el entremés del Siglo de Oro,"[1] portions of two chapters in *El Elemento Afronegroide en el Español de Puerto Rico* by Professor Manuel Alvarez Nazario of the Universidad de Puerto Rico en Mayagüez, and a paper by Dr. Alma C. Allen of Bluefield State College on "Literary Relations Between Spain and Africa." One of Dr. Allen's conclusions is that the influence of the Negro on Spanish literature is negligible. The purpose of this paper is to attempt to demonstrate that, when one considers the role the Negro plays in a number of works, his influence on Spanish literature should not be considered negligible.

Let us look first at the literature of the Middle Ages (from the early beginnings to 1406). In this literature there is a Negro in the *Auto de los Reyes Magos,* another in the "Poema de Yúsuf," and a third in one of the stories in Juan Manuel's *El Conde Lucanor.*

The Negro in the *Auto de los Reyes Magos* is Baltasar. Keeping in mind the early date of this play, we may say that the author took special pains with the characterization of this Wise Man because he conceived him as being more skeptical than the other two with regard to the star that each of them saw. We notice this in the fact that Gaspar and Melchor announce that they will be satisfied if they see the star on one more night, but Baltazar is not so easily satisfied. He declares that he must see it on three nights! We notice it also in the fact that, later on, when the Wise Men

From the *College Language Association Journal,* 9 (December, 1965), pp. 121–131. Reprinted by permission of the author and the *CLA Journal.*

come together, it is Baltazar who suggests the method to determine if the Child is actually the promised Redeemer. He suggests that they offer him gold, myrrh and incense. If the Child is an earthly king, Baltazar says, he will want the gold; if he is a mortal man, he will take the myrrh; but if he is a celestial king, he will put aside the first two offerings and accept the incense. Baltazar, then, has an important role in that play.

The "Poema de Yusúf" centers around the Biblical story of Joseph. The Negro in this poem is a slave to the merchant who purchased Joseph from his brothers. He must have been a trusted slave because the merchant places Joseph in his care. One way or another, Joseph manages to escape, and the slave goes back to look for him. When he finds him, he calls Joseph a thief and an evil person; he strikes him and knocks him senseless. The next day such a violent storm assails the caravan that the merchant concludes that someone in his retinue has committed a terrible sin. He therefore orders the guilty person to come forward and confess his evil act so that they may continue on their way. It is interesting to notice that the Negro neither cringes nor lies. He steps forward and tells his master exactly what happened and what he did. Having heard this explanation, the merchant suggests to Joseph that he take vengeance on the Negro, but Joseph declines the invitation. Then the storm abates and the caravan continues on its way.

The story in *El Conde Lucanor* which concerns us is that of "The King and the Three Tricksters." These are three men who claim that they can weave a cloth with a magical property: only those men who are legitimate sons of their fathers can see the cloth. In this story everyone from the king down claims that he can see the cloth because each one is fearful of the consequences if he were to admit that he could not see it. Some time passes. Then one day the king appears in a parade dressed in robes made from this miraculous material. Naturally, everyone is full of admiration for the exquisiteness of the king's attire, although in reality no one can see anything. Then the king comes to the place where the Negro is standing. The man looks at his king; he informs him that he does not care what people may think about his ancestry, and he adds that one of two things must be true; either he is blind or the king is riding down the street stark naked! When others watching the parade hear the Negro's remarks, first one person and then another makes the same affirmation until finally the king himself admits that he had his doubts all along about the cloth.

It seems to this writer that the roles of the Negroes in the works mentioned are not negligible.

In the literature of the Renaissance (1406 to 1516), there are kings from Manicongo, Guinea and Mandinga in the "Comedia Trofea" of Bartolomé de Torres Naharro. There is a reference to a Negro slave in a

THE NEGRO IN SPANISH LITERATURE / 31

"copla" that the courtly poet Juan Alvarez Gato addresses to a lady;[2] a Negro in "La Cárcel de Amor" by Diego de San Pedro symbolizes Despair, one of the torments that every true lover must endure to win the hand of the lady of his dreams; there are several references to the Negro among the proverbial expressions found in "Refranes que dicen las viejas tras el fuego" by Iñigo López de Mendoza, the Marqués de Santillana. There are also Negroes — but this time Negro Amazons — in the "Sergas de Esplandián" by Garci Rodríguez de Montalvo,[3] an author of *novelas de caballería* much better known for his *Amadís de Gaula*. These Negro women appear in the final battle, which is the most important adventure encountered by Esplandián, the son of Amadís, in his effort to win the hand of the incomparable Lenorina, the daughter of the emperor of Constantinople.

In this particular episode, several armies of infidels are laying siege to Constantinople, but they have failed in their repeated assaults upon the city. Then these women come along and join in the attack. The author explains that they are black but have exquisite figures, that they come from an island on the left side of the Indies called California, that they are brave and strong, and that they kill most of the men who fall into their hands. Their queen, whose name is Califa, suggests to the other chieftains that they allow her women to attempt to take the city since the men have failed thus far, and they agree. It happens that these women have brought along a special weapon: some vulture-like birds of prey which they have trained to attack and to kill their enemies but to do the Amazons no harm. The following morning, when they turn these animals loose, they fly over the walls of Constantinople and begin to kill and devour the defenders of the city. Noticing the havoc these monstrous creatures are creating, the remaining soldiers flee headlong from the walls and leave them without defenders. Then Califa calls to her allies and tells them to order their men to help her women scale the walls, but something entirely unexpected happens. The vultures cannot differentiate between the men defending the city and those who are now attempting to scale the walls. As a result they fall upon the allies of the Amazons and start killing them indiscriminately. Consequently the infidels fail again to take the city, and shortly thereafter they lift the siege and depart.

It is clear that the role of these Negro Amazons is not insignificant, for we find them revolutionizing the art of war. We find them introducing a new dimension into warfare — the use of air power!

This brings us now to the Siglo de Oro (1516 to 1681), where Negroes are much more numerous. If we examine the poetry of this period, we find that Luis de Góngora composed three poems about Negroes. In the first one, "En la Fiesta del Santísimo Sacramento," he tells about two colored girls, Clara and Juana, as they watch a procession and make comments about it. In the second one, "El Nacimiento de Cristo Nuestro Señor," another Negro girl describes enthusiastically her visit to the manger to see the Child. In the third one, "En la Fiesta de la Adoración de los Reyes," Góngora recounts the difficulties that the black king has with some shepherds when he attempts to enter the manger to worship the Child. Passing on to Francisco Gómez de Quevedo, we believe that it is sufficient simply to mention the title of his "Boda de negros" because this composition is very well and widely known. There is another poem, one described by Don Bartolomé José Galardo in his *Ensayo de una Biblioteca Española de Libros Raros y Curiosos*,[4] a poem whose title is "Granada o Descripción Historial del Insigne Reino y Ciudad Ilustrísima de Granada." According to Gallardo, this poem is about prominent citizens of Granada who distinguished themselves in various ways, and among others it includes four Negroes: a Dominican friar by the name of Cristóbal de Meneses, a lawyer whose last name was Ortiz, the very well known Juan Latino, and a lady, Catalina de Soto, who was famous for her needlework.

In the novels of the Siglo de Oro, there is no work in which a Negro plays as essential a role as Luis does in *El Celoso Extremeño* by Cervantes. Still, there are Negroes in the "Coloquio de los perros," also by Cervantes, in the "Segunda comedia de Celestina," by Feliciano de Silva,[5] in *Lazarillo de Tormes*, where we all recall Saide and Lazaro's half-brother, and in the *Aventuras del Bachiller Trapasa*, by Alonso Castillo de Solórzano.[6]

If we examine the prose literature other than the novel, all will recall, no doubt, Quevedo's chapter on Negroes called "La hora de todos." Then, there is a book bearing the very short title of *Avisos*, in which Jerónimo de Barrionuevo collected the letters that he addressed to the Dean of the Cathedral of Zaragoza in order to acquaint him with news from the capital. In five of his letters Barrionuevo includes details about a visit that an ambassador from the Congo made to Philip IV in 1658 to request Christian missionaries for his kingdom.[7] During the second half of the seventeenth century there also appeared two essays, one by Bartolomé de Albornoz,[8] the other by Fray Tomás Mercado,[9] in which the authors attacked the institution of Negro slavery vigorously. Although Negroes are not specifically mentioned in Bartolomé de las Casas's *Historia de las Indias*, the priest had already repudiated his suggestion that Negro slaves be shipped to the Indies by pointing out that the same arguments that could be presented to reject the slavery of the Indian were equally applicable to the Negro. One of his passages brings to mind Shylock's celebrated declaration on the humanity of the Jew, and we should remember that Las Casas wrote his book between 1552 and 1561, while *The Merchant of Venice* was first represented around 1596.

It is really in the theater of this period that the Negro comes into his own, because it is here that he appears in his most important roles. Disregarding all others, allow us to call attention to these four plays: *El valiente negro en Flandes,* by Andrés de Claramonte, the *Comedia famosa de Juan Latino,* by Diego Ximénez de Enciso, *El negro del mejor amo,* by Lope de Vega, and *Los hijos de la fortuna: Teágenes y Cariclea,* by Calderón de la Barca.

The play by Claramonte, *El valiente negro en Flandes,* is about Juan de Mérida, a Negro who covers himself with glory while serving with the Spanish army in the Low Countries. No doubt the author exaggerates. Still, this is what he has Juan de Mérida do: first, he takes two enemy soldiers prisoners. Thereupon the Duke of Alba, the Spanish commander-in-chief, makes him a sergeant. Then, he kills a Flemish captain in single combat; the duke now makes him a captain. Finally, he steals into the enemy camp, makes a prisoner of the Duke of Orange, the Flemish general, and leads him back to the Spanish lines. Of course this brings the campaign to a victorious conclusion. Shortly afterwards the king of Spain makes Juan a general and elevates him to the nobility.

It is probably not necessary to discuss at length the play by Ximénez de Enciso about Juan Latino because all of us are acquainted with him. We know that he was born in Africa, that he grew up in the household of El Gran Capitán Gonzalo Fernández de Córdoba, that as a child he accompanied the son of the Duke of Sesa and carried his books for him, that he profited much more from the study of said books than did his young master, that he became a famous and respected professor, and that he married the beautiful Ana de Carlobal. The principal liberty that the author takes with the facts about Juan Latino's life is that in the play the duke does not grant his slave his liberty, contending that he derives much greater satisfaction from being known as Juan's master than from any of the exploits which made his family historically famous.

Lope Félix de Vega Carpio presents Negroes in a number of his works. The work that we have selected for discussion is remarkable because it begins with events which take place before the birth of the hero and comes to a close with an incident that takes place after his death. In *El negro del mejor amo,* Lope tells the story of Antiobo, a Negro prince. In the first act, we learn that he is the son of Dulimán, king of Algeria, and Sofonisba, an extraordinarily attractive black princess. The problem here is that Antiobo is supposed to be a Moslem, but he worries his father because of the unusual concern that he displays for the Christian captives in the country. To determine definitely what his son's religious inclinations really are, Dulimán dispatches him with a fleet of Algerian warships to support the Turks in an assault upon the island of Sardinia, which is inhabited by

Christians. When the fleet reaches the island, Antiobo's Christian beliefs assert themselves, for he takes the side of the Sardinians. With his assistance, the islanders repulse the Turkish attack and Antiobo settles down to spend the rest of his life among the Sardinians performing good deeds. Shortly after his death, the Turks return for another assault on the island, but Antiobo's body helps the defenders to repulse their enemies once more.

This brings us now to the play by Calderón, to *Los hijos de la fortuna: Teágenes y Cariclea*. In the September 1962 issue of the *College Language Association Journal,* Dr. Hobart Jarrett wrote:

The learned Burton also cites a curious reference. Writing of pre-natal influences, Burton informs us that "Persina, that Ethiopian queen in Heliodorus, by seeing the picture of Perseus and Andromeda, instead of a blackamoor, was brought to bed of a fair, white child."

The Burton referred to is, of course, Robert Burton; the book in question is his *Anatomy of Melancholy.* As far as we know, no English dramatist has ever based a play on this plot, but that is exactly what Calderón de la Barca did.

In this play, Persina is the Negro queen of Ethiopia who gives birth to a girl who is so fair that she resolves to get rid of her for fear of what her husband and her subjects might suspect. Therefore, she takes the newborn baby, places it in a crib along with a chest full of jewels and abandons it at the foot of a cliff. Presently a wealthy Ethiopian comes along, finds the crib and takes the little creature home. The child grows up and becomes a stunningly beautiful young woman. Her adopted father takes this girl, Cariclea, to the Temple of Apollo in Delphus for safekeeping because an oracle has predicted that her true identity will not be known until the day when she is sacrificed. To make a long story short, Cariclea winds up in Egypt exactly at the time when war is declared between Ethiopia and Egypt over the rights to some mines. Before setting forth to do battle, Persina, the queen of the Ethiopians, prays to her goddess Andromeda and vows to sacrifice to her the first enemy that she takes prisoner if Andromeda grants her the victory. Sure enough, Persina wins the war and Cariclea is the first person that she takes prisoner. Remembering her vow, she prepares to sacrifice the girl to her goddess, but at that very moment the wealthy Ethiopian who discovered the crib comes forward, recognizes Cariclea as his adopted daughter, and tells Persina that she cannot sacrifice her because she is not an Egyptian, that she is an Ethiopian child whom he found abandoned in a crib. Now Persina confesses that the child was actually her daughter and she explains why she abandoned her. When an Ethiopian scientist hears her explanation, he informs her that he can account scientifically for the child's fair complexion. His explanation is that the queen gazed upon Andromeda's countenance so often that this caused her to give birth to a fair child. We have called attention to some works in Spanish literature up to the end of the Siglo de Oro in which Negroes appear. Although the works mentioned are few, we hope that they are sufficient to support the contention that, in view of the roles that Negroes play in them, their influence is not negligible.

NOTES

1. *Hispania* (March 1961), pp. 55–65.
2. "Cancionero Castellano del Siglo XV," Ordenado por R. Foulché-Delbosc, *Nueva Biblioteca de Autores Españoles,* Vol. 19 (Madrid, 1912), pp. 223–224.
3. *Biblioteca de Autores Españoles,* Vol. 40 (Madrid, 1950), pp. 403–561.
4. Bartolomé José Gallardo, *Ensayo de una Biblioteca Española de Libros Raros y Curiosos,* Vol. I (Madrid, 1888), Columnas 865–874.
5. Feliciano de Silva, "Segunda comedia de Celestina," con introducción por D. José Antonio de Balenchana, *Colección de Libros Raros o Curiosos,* Vol. IX (Madrid, 1874).
6. Alonso Castillo de Solórzano, *Las Aventuras del Bachiller Trapaza,* Edición, prólogo y notas de Agustín del Campo (Madrid, 1949).
7. Jerónimo de Barrionuevo, *Avisos* (1654–1658), Precede una noticia de la vida y escritos del autor por A. Paz y Melia, Vol. IV (Madrid, 1892), pp. 101–102; 110–111; 138; 147 and 162.
8. Bartolomé de Albornoz, "De la esclavitud," *Biblioteca de Autores Españoles,* Vol. LXV (Madrid, 1873), pp. 232–233.
9. José Antonio Saco, *Historia de la esclavitud de la raza africana en el Nuevo Mundo y en especial en los países americo-hispanos,* Prólogo de Fernando Ortiz, Vol. II (Habana, 1938), pp. 80–82.

CARTER G. WOODSON

Attitudes of the Iberian Peninsula
(in Literature)

Spanish and Portuguese literature, like the history of these people, early
showed attitudes toward the Negro. Following the example of historians,
moreover, this first notice was merely in allusions and remnants of myths
and fables like those connected with the Song of Roland, the Knights of
the Round Table, the Holy Grail, and the Cid. Some black knight was
pictured in most of these circles to give them color.[1] As Negroes did not
come into Iberia in large numbers prior to the middle of the fifteenth
century, however, no particular notice was taken of such an element in
that out-of-the-way part of the world. True enough, as well-authenticated
accounts prove, Negroes had touched the Peninsula just as they had other
parts of Europe bordering upon the Mediterranean, but such infusions of
Negro blood were so infrequent as to undergo dilution to the extent that
it was not very noticeable prior to the period of discovery ushered in by
Prince Henry of Portugal.

Drawn immediately into the circle of those sent to discover, explore
and settle the New World, the Negro became a topic occasionally mentioned in historical literature. The efforts of the *predictors,* and especially of Bartolomé de las Casas, projected the Negro further into the fore-
ground, and so did the frequent use of imported Africans by the *Conquistadores.* In addition to the works of Bartolomé de las Casas, already cited,
one should note also José Antonio Saco's *Historia de la Esclavitud;* Gonzalo Fernández de Oviedo's *Historia General;* Herrera's *Historia General;*

From the *Journal of Negro History*, 20, no. 2 (April, 1935), pp. 190–
243. Copyright by the Association for the Study of Negro Life and History, Inc. Reprinted by permission of the ASALH and the *Journal of
Negro History.*

Bernard Díaz del Castillo's *Conquista de Nueva España;* and Pedro de Casteñada's "Account of the Expedition to Cibola which took place in the year 1540," a translation in the series *Spanish Explorers in the Southern United States.* Negroes in various numbers are noted in these enterprises in commendable roles, but the most picturesque figures in this literature have already been noted above.

The first important role played by the Negro in Spanish fiction appears in *El Celoso Extremeño,* or "The Jealous Estramaduran," by Cervantes, the author of *Don Quijote.* Briefly told, "The Jealous Estramaduran" is the story of a prodigal son who wasted his wealth in riotous living and finally went to the Indies to recover his fortune. He finally decided to marry a young woman who happened to be of a poor family although of noble birth.

Insanely jealous of the woman (knowing that in his advanced age he would not strikingly appeal to her and that she would have a natural preference for some younger man), he established her in a castle in which she was kept practically as a prisoner. Into this enclosure were to come no additional males except Luis, a Negro eunuch, employed to attend the old man's mule; and the African was daily locked in so as to have no contact with the young wife. She was attended by a duena, assisted by two Negro women servants and four white slave girls branded in their faces.

Loaysa disguised himself as a lame beggar and, through the keyhole of the apartment in which the Negro eunuch was kept, the youth so charmed the servant with his music from the street that the latter without a key effected some way of lifting the door from the hinges and permitted the adventurer to enter his apartment in the loft. Becoming the instructor of the Negro, the musician flattered him with the thought that he was progressing much more rapidly than he was and left him a guitar, upon which he could play certain tunes at an hour when they could not be heard by the old man.

The point to be noted here with respect to the Negro is that the author emphasizes in the play the Negro's love of music and his aptitude in this art. The play turns upon this particular point. In the street from which the young man, disguised as a beggar, was trying with his companions to win over the Negro eunuch, the story says, "The boys all made a ring around him when he sang and Luis, the Negro, enchanted by the virote's music, would have given one of his hands to be able to open the door, and listen to him at his ease, such is the fondness for music inherent in the Negro race." Playing upon this trait of the Negro, Loaysa says further to Luis, "Among my pupils I have three Negroes, slaves to three aldermen, whom I have taught so well that they are fit to sing and play at any dance or in any tavern." At another point, Loaysa is pictured as "singing a sprightly ditty with such good effect that the Negro was in ecstasy and felt as if the time for opening the door would never arrive." It looked very much like "social equality," too, when as he entered, "Loaysa embraced his pupil, kissed him on the cheek, and immediately put into his hands a big jar of wine, a box of preserves and other sweet things with which his wallet was well stored."

At the time of the interesting party finally staged in the household, however, the author apparently puts the two Negro women down at the end of the social ladder, for he says, "After all the women, from the lady of the house down to the negresses, had thus gratified their eyes, Loaysa took his guitar, and played a song more bewitchingly than ever." At another point the author says, "The appointed hour having arrived, all the domestics, great and small, black and white, repaired to the turning-box, longing to see the *señor músico* fairly within their seraglio." Yet in the arrangement of the household the author speaks of the owner as providing it with four white slave girls whom he branded in the face, but the two Negro women, occupying apparently the same status, were not thus treated as if they were cattle. In the next place Guiomar, the Negro sent to watch over the old man lest he might wake up during this party, is made to talk in a brogue not much better than that spoken by Negroes trying to use other modern languages; and when the Negro all but breaks up the party with the false alarm that the old man had awakened, the wrath expressed would seem to leave the impression of the Negro's inclination toward mendacity.

And the author plays up again the Negro's love of music when as a result of this alarm Luis is presented as running, hugging his guitar, and he "hid himself in his loft, where he huddled up under the bed-clothes, sweating with terror; in spite of which he could not forbear from tinkling the guitar from time to time, so inordinate — may Satanas confound him! — was his love of music."

Cervantes, however, did not have as a dominant factor in his make-up any sense of depreciation of the Negro, as certain allusions in his writings may seem to indicate. He was rather hard on the Moors, just as most Spanish writers were; and, having suffered from capture and enslavement among their kindred in North Africa, he may have had an additional reason for this attitude. His language does not show the same attitude toward the Negroes, some of whom were mixed with the Moors. The word "Negro" was used in those days as we use "black" today without any thought of race. As a Spanish author says in his own language, "Es color infausta y triste, y como tal vsamos desta palabra, diziendo: negra ventura, etc." (Covarrubias). And we find "la negra orden de casualleria" in *Don Quijote,* I, iii. It is known, however, that Cervantes keenly appreciated the contribution of Juan Latino, the most distinguished Negro in Spain at that time. In a poem prefixed to *Don Quijote* the author took note of this scholarly figure, as did many others among his contemporaries. The lines thus giving the famous linguist honorable mention are:

> Since Heaven it hath not pleased on thee
> Deep erudition to bestow,
> Or black Latino's gift of tongues,

In his play *La Dama Boba*, Lope de Vega, the most productive of all Spanish writers, takes occasion also to refer to Juan Latino's status and courtship. Juan Latino is otherwise known to fame. In thus rising in the world he owed much to Don John of Austria, whom he did not forget. "A vast number of tributes were paid by contemporary men of letters to Don John of Austria," says George Ticknor in his *History of Spanish Literature* (II, p. 582) "but among them none is more curious than a Latin poem in two books containing seventeen or eighteen hundred hexameters, the work of a Negro, who had been brought as an infant from Africa, and who by his learning rose to be Professor of Latin and Greek in the school attached to the cathedral of Granada. He is the same person noted by Cervantes as 'el Negro Juan Latino,' in a poem prefixed to the *Don Quijote*. His volume of Latin verses on the birth of Ferdinand, the son of Philip II, on Pope Pius V, on Don John of Austria, and on the city of Granada, making above a hundred and sixty pages in small quarto, printed at Granada in 1573, is not only one of the rarest books in the world, but is one of the most remarkable illustrations of the intellectual faculties and possible accomplishments of the African race."

Juan Latino himself says he was brought to Spain from Ethiopia, and until his manumission was a slave to the grandson of the famous Gonsalvo de Córdoba. "His Latin verse is respectable," says Ticknor, "and, from his singular success as a scholar, he was commonly called Joannes Latinus, a *sobriquet* under which he is frequently mentioned. He was respectably married to a lady of Granada, who fell in love with him, as Eloise did with Abelard, while he was teaching her; and after his death, which occurred later than 1573, his wife and children erected a monument to his memory in the church of Sta. Ana, in that city, inscribing it with an epitaph, in which he is styled "Filius Aethiopum, prolesque nigerrima patrum."[2]

There is a play entitled *Juan Latino* by Diego Ximénez de Enciso, in the second volume of the *Comedias Escogidas* (Madrid, 1652), which gives a full sketch of the Latin scholar. "In the first act," says Ticknor, "he is a slave of the Duke of Sesa, ill enough treated, kicked about and cuffed.

In the second, he is tutor to Doña Ana de Carlobal, sister to an ecclesiastic of rank, and makes love to her through his Spanish verses, and in other ways after the Spanish fashion. In the third, he rises to distinction; obtains his chair in the University; and, favored by Don Juan of Austria, is enfranchised by the Duke of Sesa, who, however, manumits him very reluctantly, on the ground that it is his great glory to hold so distinguished a man as his property."

The hero is next favored by Don Juan of Austria, who showers many honors upon him and uses his good offices to induce the Duke to manumit Juan. The attitude is further shown by the eulogy on Juan Latino by his distinguished friend in the following sonnet:

> I am the son of a slave. I was born in Baena,
>   where I first learned the alphabet;
>   I grew up seeking the true goal,
>   the prize which heaven offers for virtue.
> No burden was my pleasant task
>   of a prebendary of Granada,
>   with Orpheus, Mars, Cicero, Homer,
>   in voice, in arms, in Latin, in poetry.
> I was a professor, excellent in Greek
>   and finally, distinguished man; then from this position
>   I became a distinguished tax-collector.
> And as Ancient Rome designated Adrian
>   as eminent in calling him Greek,
>   noble Spain called me Latin.

"It may not be amiss here to add," says Ticknor, "that another Negro is celebrated in a play, written with skill in good Castilian, and claiming, at the end, to be founded in fact. It is called *El valiente negro en Flandes*, by Andrés de Claramonte, actor and playwright, and is found in Tom. XXXI, 1638, of the *Collection of Comedies* printed at Barcelona and Saragossa. The Negro in question, however, was not, like Juan Latino, a native African, but was a slave born in Merida, and was distinguished only as a soldier, serving with great honor under the Duke of Alva, and enjoying the favor of that severe general."

Lope de Vega, as already herein referred to, thus brought the Negro into his writings. In most cases these were ordinary allusions of no particular literary significance but without prejudice. He frequently referred to the black saints and occasionally played up persons of this color in his comedies. In the discussion of the attitude of Lope de Vega, however, one must not be misled by the frequency of his mentioning the *Negro* in his writings. The way the Negro is thereby introduced is more important.

In Lope de Vega neither the Moor nor the Jew of this time measured up to the level of the Spaniard. They were not militant Christians. The Negro, with less mention than these other foreigners on the stage, is treated more sympathetically. Lope de Vega had a special tondness for Negro music and dance, and he frequently introduced black characters to dramatize the achievements of the race in these spheres. In the closing of the *Nacimiento de Cristo* (the Birth of Christ) he introduces with splendid effect the three kings preceded by dances of Gypsies and Negroes. In *La Vitoria de la honra*, Anton, Tiznado, and a Negro woman soloist, together with a chorus of beautiful voices, intersperse the production in most entertaining fashion.

In the play called *El Mayor rey de los reyes* (King of Kings) we find the Negro given a still more prominent place by Lope de Vega. Among the kings who, according to the biblical story of the Magi, came to do honor to the Babe of Bethlehem was the Negro King Melchor, frequently mentioned elsewhere in other modern literature and art of Europe. Along with King Melchor appear Butifar, Zaydan, a black queen, and a priest, all Negroes, who figure conspicuously throughout this play on a parity with others.

The next writer of consequence to project the Negro into literature was Calderón. Calderón's attitude toward the subordinated elements of the social order may be defined as still more favorable than that of his distinguished predecessors. With respect to the Negro, Calderón's writings not only show allusions to color with reference to Moors in such plays as *El Gran Príncipe de Fez, Don Baltasar de Loyola* and *La Niña de Gómez Arias*, but he devotes one play especially to the Negro in which black persons play important parts. This is his *Sabila del Oriente y Gran Reina de Sabá.*

This play is based upon the famous theme of the contacts of Solomon and the Queen of Sheba. It is at the same time a contrast of one Oriental culture with that of another, or the contrast of the civilization of the Hamites with that of the Semites. The play gives a contemporary conception of the ancient history of these people with, of course, the exaggeration that a thing of this sort naturally would have on the stage. It belongs to the old classic drama. Nothing of any great consequence is added to the story of this visit of one sovereign to the other, but it is made sufficiently romantic to give further ground for the claim of the Abyssinians' being the descendants of the offspring of Solomon and the Queen of Sheba. It should be noted, too, that the important characters in this play were not drawn exclusively from Ethiopia and Judea. In the drama one finds Hiram, King of Tyre; Candaces, King of Egypt; Libio, King of Palmyra; and Mandinga, together with a Negro *gracioso,* and such Negro women as Irifile, Casimira, and Irene. In conformity to the classic drama, the author has conceived these as types into whose mouths he puts his own words.

In another of Calderón's plays, *Los hijos de la fortuna, Teágenes y Cariclea*, we have the Negro also occupying a conspicuous place in an international drama. This is an effort to bring into play the conflict of the culture of the Orient with that of the Occident. Here one sees the Ethiopian, the Egyptian, and the Greek in action. The play follows the rule of classicism. While Teágenes and Cariclea are the chief characters in the story, the Negro is projected into it sufficiently to give the drama color. All of the Negroes brought into the picture, then, are not servants. The author makes Idaspe, a black man, speak for himself as an aristocrat, saying, "I am a noble Satrap of Ethiopia, who, elevated by blood and fortune, find few equals." There is also Persina, the Negro Queen of Ethiopia, with black servants, nymphs and musicians, who in their display of talent help to establish the claim of the Negro to achievement in music even at that early day. Here Calderón is following the example of Lope de Vega in thus continuing Negro music and dance on the Spanish stage. Evidently the Negro in the histrionic sphere in Europe reached his first high level in Spain during its golden age of the seventeenth century.

The details of *Los hijos de la fortuna* have no particular concern for us here. We are especially interested in the way these black characters were staged to portray the status and history of that country in the drama in which Ethiopians and Egyptians of diluted Negro blood play their parts along with Greeks. The Greeks greatly admired the Ethiopians as the leaders of ancient culture and referred to them as being so highly favored as to feast among the gods. While one does not find here the same picture as that set forth in such history of the Greeks as that recorded by Herodotus and in the poems of Homer and Aeschylus, he does get sufficient glimpses of it to warrant the conclusion that in ancient times the Negro was one of the important factors in making an advanced world culture. This Oriental civilization was taken over by the Europeans who went into the Crusades as half savages and returned from the East with sufficient enlightenment to civilize their continent.

After the great masters of Spanish literature had passed out about the middle of the seventeenth century the literature of that country declined to a low level. About one century later, however, near the middle of the eighteenth century, we find better beginnings and, therefore, a literature more representative of a modern nation. Yet, inasmuch as Spain, like some other countries, had entered upon the program of ruthless exploitation of its colonies with the use of laboring elements, most of whom were free people of color and Negro slaves, the Negro in that literature did not fare so well. Much bitterness developed thereafter with respect to these elements, not because they were black but because they were the victims of a selfish colonial policy. In the production of Spanish realists, therefore, we find sometimes allusions which indicate that the Negro was regarded very much as he was in any other European country with such connections. The Negro is not frequently mentioned, but the attitude is curtly expressed.

In the case of *El Moro Expósito,* by Angel de Saavedra or the Duke of Rivas, we find such an allusion. One of the characters referred to in the poem as a Negro is denounced as an infamous black who should be dead. In another play, *Guzmán el Bueno,* by Don Antonio Gil y Zárate, the blacks are brought into the equation along with the Moors. Here the theme comes also from the days of Islam.

References to the Negro in modern Spanish writings grow less and less and tend to classify the race as unequal to the European. For example, in Don Manuel Bretón's *La Independencia* the word *Negro* is used to denote a very brown or black color of a member of a lower social order. In *El Trovador,* Antonio García Gutierez, with the same attitude, makes an uncomplimentary allusion to the Negro. He would have the term mean gloom, as in the *Negra estrella.* In this way he makes use of the folktale of the *Cuero Negro,* on which is based Edgar Allan Poe's "Raven." The presence of this dark species is considered as indicating misfortune or foreboding evil, which tends to make the word *Negro* become more and more synonymous with that which is impure, uninviting, and undesirable. Whether this use of the term indicates the attitude of Gutierez or merely something which he borrowed from another literature is not clear. It should be remarked that this allusion to the "Raven" is found in all great literatures, including those of the Mesopotamians, the Greeks, and the Romans. It may be added here, too, that the word *Negro* was a name given in Spain to the moderates of the Cortés of 1820 by the "exaltados," who had provoked the provincial revolution.

The same sort of attitude is observed in Fernán Caballero's *La Familia de Alvareda.* To illustrate a point the author reverts to the proverb characterizing one in a peculiarly difficult situation out of which there are apparently ways of escape none of which can be used. The illustration is the folk tale of a little Negro enamored of another man's wife who finally informs her husband of the African's unsolicited attentions. The husband, in collusion with the aggrieved wife, plans a tryst for the ardent lover with his wife in a room with three doors. The Negro appears upon the scene, overjoyed and laden with numerous gifts with which he would gladden the heart of his now willing conquest. No sooner has he taken his seat and begins to approach the wife with affection, however, than the husband seizes upon the little Negro and belabors him so terribly that, although there are three doors in the room, he is not given time to escape by any.

An American editor, commenting on this novel, refers to this tale as one of the weaknesses of Caballero's story because it adds nothing to the narrative, and serves merely as a diversion which causes the movement to lag. This criticism, however, seems a little severe, but it may be explained by the usual bias of the Nordic commentator who would hardly consider any such notice of a Negro as in good taste. Doubtless if the allusion had been to a Negro in the role of a clown rather than as paying court to a Spanish lady it would not have been thus noticed by the fastidious editor.

Juan Eugenio Hartzenbusch also stands among those who could not escape bias. His attitude with respect to the Negro is best shown in his very popular *Los Amantes de Teruel.* This is a drama of love in which the hero, a captive in prison, is being made love to by a dusky Moorish sultana. He resists the sultana's entreaties because of his belief in his superiority as a Nordic. He pines for the absent blonde heroine, although she is besieged by many other suitors. The heroine, finally convinced that the hero is dead or unworthy on some other account, accepts one of her many suitors. In the meantime the hero gets away from the dusky sultana only to fall into the clutches of robbers. Finally he arrives at the home of the heroine too late, and the lovers commit suicide.

The point in the play of Hartzenbusch is the contrast of one race with the other. The dusky Arab of diluted African blood was voluptuous, licentious. The Nordic of the race to which Hartzenbusch belonged, for his father was a German, although his mother was a native of Spain and he developed in that country, was inherently superior. In other words, in spite of itself it is almost impossible for literature to be other than racially biased. Europe was feeling its superiority over the Orient which had civilized it, and this must now creep into the thought of the best thinkers of the time. They thus used their literary productions for propaganda.

In the case of Pedro Antonio Alarcón we see further evidence of the attitude toward the Negro in the literature of that country. In his blood-and-thunder dime novel, *El Final de Norma,* he makes a Negro the companion of one of the most important characters. Just why this Negro should be taken out of his milieu to go as far north as Greenland and Iceland requires a stretch of the imagination of which only Alarcón himself is capable. And yet this Negro brought into the story does not develop as a character. In one case the author refers to his hiding *su caja de dientes.* The Negro is also presented as lacking even in sufficient knowledge to speak a modern language.

The same attitude, however, did not appear in the writings of all Spanish authors of this time. In spite of themselves some of them had an African temperament and could not easily get rid of that influence. In the case of Vicente Medina, a native of Murcia in southern Spain, one of the most Africanized portions of that land, this color is evident in his writings.

Sometimes it appears in the case of others where it is not expected. "The Tribute to the Dark Beauty," by Francisco Villaespesa, is a case in evidence. He wrote thus:

> If I am lost in the world,
> seek me in Andalucia.
> . . . . .
> there you will see me talking
> with the prettiest dark beauty
> of those who show their eyes
> across a mantilla.
> [tran. by L. A. Warren]

It should be noted, moreover, that some liberal movements did have the same effect in Spain as they had elsewhere. Be it said to the credit of Spain that some ten years before *Uncle Tom's Cabin* was brought out, Gertrudis Gómez de Avellaneda, essentially a Cuban, wrote and published in Spain in 1839 a novel called *Sab,* in which she attacked slavery with much vigor. Lacking some of the merits of her American compeer, she did not arouse such popular interest as did Harriet Beecher Stowe, but she did express her indignation against the abuses of the system; and this work is still referred to as showing literary merit.

Into Spain, however, came the crimes of the exploitation which moved other parts of the world. Spain naturally felt bitter when, in spite of her struggle to maintain her empire, she saw it gradually taken away in the movement for independence in the Latin American republics. The black people themselves in these various republics were the oppressed not because they were Negroes, but because they had once been slaves and had not been able to rise to the level of the exploiting class. In most of these cases, therefore, Spain naturally crushed the aspirations of those whom we call people of African descent. Some few of these, like Enriques Días, who fought with Portugal, helped to maintain the old order, but others resorted to revolutionary efforts. Gabriel de la Concepción Valdés, called "Plácido," distinguished himself in writings such as "Jicotencal," "Despidida a mi madre," and finally "Plegaria a Dios," which he recited when he was on the way to his execution in 1844. He, it was said, had tried to stir up a revolution of the blacks against Spain, but investigation has never revealed more than a general suspicion on account of which this promising author went to a martyr's grave. He was, then, the forerunner of Antonio Maceo.

We are not surprised, then, to observe that in traveling through Spain today one finds no evidence of racial discrimination based upon color. There are cases of persons being referred to as Negroes if they happen to be black or nearly so, but without prejudice. Spain evidently, then, is one of the countries which has been saved from the evils of race prejudice.

NOTES

1. Pedro Bohigas Balaguer, *Los textos españoles y gallego-portugueses de la demanda del Santo Grail* (Madrid, 1925); *Journal of Negro History*, 18, pp. 225–245.
2. Antonio, *Bib. Nov.*, Tom. 1, p. 716. *Don Quixote*, ed. Clemencin, Tom L. p. ix, note. Andreas Schottus, in his *Hispaniae Bibliotheca sive de Academiis et Bibliothecis* (1608), speaking of the city of Granada, says: "Hic Joannes Latinus Aethiops, (res prodigiosa) nostra tempestate rhetoricam per multos annos publice docuit, juventutemque institui, et poema edidit in victoriam Joannis Austriaci navalem" (p. 29).

VALAUREZ B. SPRATLIN

The Negro in Spanish Literature

Toward the end of the fifteenth century, as a result of Portuguese incursions along the coast of Guinea, the wharves of Seville saw black people among the cargo unloaded. Most of them were destined to serve as domestics, for with the discovery of America, agriculture and the ruder occupations were abandoned amid the get-rich-quick excitement. Consequently the Negro slave in Spain enjoyed an advantageous position that in many cases made possible the cultivation of what talents he possessed.

This new element in Spanish society was bound to play its role in the national literature, and we are not surprised to find Negroes among the motley procession that was the stupendous creation of the literary genius of Renaissance Spain. Spanish literature, from the beginning, has been essentially realistic in spirit, and the literature of the Golden Age presents the Negro as he was — illiterate, often, and uncouth, but a human being, withal. Indeed, there is no hesitation before miscegenation; in *Lazarillo de Tormes,* the first of the novels of roguery, the stepfather of the hero is black (a character left out of one American edition of the work). He is a rascal, but no more disreputable than the other characters of this scintillating satire, which spares neither gentleman nor priest.

The black buffoon is not missing in the early Spanish dramas. This type, however, simply marked the first step in a literary evolution that has come to produce a type like the hero of Insúa's contemporary novel, *The Negro Whose Soul Was White.* In the sixteenth century Lope de Rueda

From the *Journal of Negro History* (January, 1934), pp. 62–71. Copyright 1934 by the Association for the Study of Negro Life and History, Inc. Reprinted by permission of Estrelda Spratlin Gray, the ASALH and the *Journal of Negro History.*

diverts his audiences with the facile humor of black folks whose linguistic difficulties are as amusing as their pranks. In the drama *Los engaños*, a tender display of maternal instinct on the part of the black Guiomar contrasts with her ludicrous illiteracy and indecency of speech. In *Eufemia, the Dark Domestic*, Eulalia, during an interview with her lover Polo, is suffering from the ill effects of a bleach applied to her hair; nothing daunted, she asks Polo to procure for her a similar cosmetic for her hands. But the lover is quite content with the lady as she is, and tells her that a white face could be no dearer to him. Eulalia explains that although her face is dark, her body is as smooth as velvet. In the light of latter-day criticism, the lady's reply is significant of something more than the coarseness that characterized the theater of that time. Values are constantly being revised and a favorite thought among the intellectual vanguard of contemporary Spain is that the sensuality imputed to the Moors and darker races in general is saner and healthier than the ascetic, life-denying Christian ideal that has peopled Spain with nuns and anchorites.

We shall dismiss this flippant treatment of the Negro in the earlier years of the Spanish drama to consider briefly a remarkable presentation of the black man's cause by the greatest of all Spanish satirists, Quevedo. After reading "La hora de todos," written about 1640, we conclude that what seemed merciless misanthropy in this dyspeptic writer was in reality righteous indignation before social evils. In this phantasy of Quevedo, we see Jupiter chiding Fortune for her caprices. A council of the gods decides that at a given hour, justice shall be established in the world and every man will find himself with what he deserves. After the hour has struck, enslaved Negroes gather from all parts of the world to plot their freedom. Their spokesman is an old patriarch who sees in his complexion a motive for pride rather than shame, being, as it is, the effect of "the embrace of the greatest beauty, the sun." If the Negroes are a blot among the whites, the latter are a stain among the blacks. Quevedo then proposes the blending of the races; the black blood, he says, will improve the white, for "white is the color of the Flemings, Germans, and French who keep the world in turmoil." What a prophet was Quevedo! Shall we pass his remedy on to Geneva, now that all others, it seems, have failed?

These, however, are interpretations of black folk by writers of the other race. What has the Spanish Negro himself accomplished? In military affairs there are the exploits of Juan de Mérida, "The Valiant Negro of Flanders" and hero of a play by Andrés de Claramonte; in painting there are the works of Sebastián Gómez and Juan Pareja; and in literature there are the career and works of Juan Latino.

The story of Juan de Mérida is more legendary than real, yet in view of the essentially historical nature of the play by Claramonte, we conclude that its argument is founded on fact. Here we have a full-length portrait of a hero, who by virtue of his valor becomes general under the Duke of Alba, the dreaded Spanish leader of the Dutch Wars. So enthusiastic does the author become as he narrates his deeds, that he does violence to fact by having him capture William of Orange alone and single-handed. Mesonero Romanos tells us that the drama was highly successful in its day and that the author promised a second part, which was done, it seems, by a colleague, Vicente Guerrero, whose works are not extant.

Sebastián Gómez and Juan Pareja belong to the history of art, and I shall dismiss them with a recollection of the pride and joy that came over me as I viewed their works in Seville and Madrid. Who can doubt the artistic capacity of the Negro, when a slave like Pareja can surreptitiously develop a technic that has been mistaken for that of Velázquez, his master, who, according to many critics, is the greatest painter of all times?

The climax of the Negro's achievement in Spain is the career of Juan Latino, whose Latin verses entitle him to a prominent place among the Spanish humanists of the sixteenth century. According to the internal evidence of *The Austriad,* his masterpiece, he was born in Africa and sold into slavery in Spain at an early age. It was his good fortune to serve in the household of Gonzalo of Córdoba, Spain's greatest warrior. Indeed, the encouragement that the young slave received in the cultivation of his talents makes us think that Old Spain was as generous as she was arrogant. Once his aptitudes became known, Juan was put to school, where admiring fellow-students dubbed him "Latino." All Granada paid him homage; in his classroom he numbered both high and lowly among his students; one of Granada's fairest became his bride; and John of Austria, son of Charles the Fifth, invited him often to dine at the royal table.

It was to commemorate this friendship with John of Austria that the slave-poet wrote his masterpiece. The victory over the Turks at Lepanto had made John the hero of Christian Europe, and Juan Latino wrote a Latin poem of epic proportions as his tribute. Should the student who has passed his Virgil be given to vainglory over his Latinity, let him try *The Austriad* of the black poet as a lesson in self-abasement. Under the pen of the slave of Granada the Latin language was like metal in the molds of Cellini; it could twist itself into phantastic shapes no less intricate than beautiful.

Let us now turn from Spain to Spanish America in this rapid survey. The sun long ago passed the meridian over there, but it has hardly reached noon-day in the new continent, and the Negro will do well to watch the play of light and shade in the Latin countries to the south of us. Early in the sixteenth century Negro slaves were introduced in large numbers into Spanish America. The priest, Bartolomé de las Casas, cognizant of the inability of the Indians to endure the hardships of slavery, advocated their substitution by Negroes. In justice to his dubious humanitarianism it must be admitted that he later regretted such counsel. The result of this substitution was that a vast field of action was opened up to the Negro; on this western stage his achievements are more varied than on the eastern.

In the first place, there is the spectacle of the slave endeavoring to break his chains. In 1549 the Negro Felipillo, with other slaves, fled from the Archipelago of las Perlas to a citadel near the gulf of San Miguel. Others from the city of Panama followed them. They were unable to resist their former masters, and Francisco Carreno, after burning their buildings, took thirty of them back to Panama, where one was drawn and quartered as a lesson to the others.

In 1552 a slave Miguel, to escape punishment, fled from the mines of San Felipe de Buria in Venezuela and, together with some one hundred and fifty Negroes and Indians inspired by his rude eloquence, took refuge in the mountains. He, too, could not hold out against the enemy; after his death in an encounter his followers were either executed or enslaved.

And now, as a foil to the pusillanimous Emperor Jones and his mock Caribbean kingdom, let me present King Bayano of Panama and his court of fugitive slaves. The following passage from *The History of Venezuela* by Fray Pedro de Aguado describes their purpose:

In those same days the citizens of Panama and Nombre de Dios, and especially the merchants, were living in great fear because some time before, many Negro slaves, weary of the servitude and captivity in which their masters held them, had fled to the most intricate part of the mountains for the purpose of preserving their liberty or dying in its behalf. Here in the mountains they had constructed a kind of city-fortress, and leaving in it the women, children and others not serviceable in war, the most valiant and daring sallied forth to plunder on the highway that crosses the Panama beginning at Nombre de Dios.

The historian describes how they attacked caravans of merchants on the road and, after a general slaughter, carried off the booty. On one occasion, the leader of a foraging expedition generously spared the defeated and allowed them to continue their journey with a part of their goods. Unable to protect the road from such incursions, the governor of Panama decided to attack Bayano, the chief of the insurgent slaves, in his mountain citadel. The Negro had chosen wisely the site for his fortress, for the Spaniards found it impregnable. A truce having been arranged, the fugitives enjoyed complete freedom of action. Later, however, perfidy accomplished what martial prowess could not. The Spaniards had encamped on a plain below the mountain citadel, and following the armistice the opposing factions had fraternized freely, the blacks believing Spanish protestations of friendship. The crafty Orsua, leader of the Spaniards, arranged a banquet to which he invited Bayano and his retinue. The wine for the feast was drugged. Before lethargy had overcome the guests, each was ushered into an antechamber to receive a present from Orsua. As one stretched out his hand to receive his gift in the guise of a cloak, he was fatally stabbed by a dagger concealed under the garment. He shouted treason, but to no avail. Spanish soldiers rushed from concealment to seize Bayano and those of his men who had not already been overcome by the wine. The citadel, thus left defenseless, became easy prey to the enemy. The blacks fled but, under promise of safety, returned and were conducted to a settlement near Panama. King Bayano was carried to the viceroy in Lima, who loaded him with gifts and then sent him to Seville, where he spent the remainder of his days, a pensioner of the crown.

Centuries pass and the South American Negro is no longer a slave, but a citizen and patriot, fighting side by side with the whites in defense of liberty and right. The first half of the nineteenth century sees General Barcala winning laurels in the hectic Brazilian scene and then aiding the Argentine patriots in combating the armies of the dictator Rosas. At the end of the century Antonio Maceo wins international renown as the Cuban patriot whose military genius plays its part in bringing Spanish domination to an end in the island.

I regret that time does not permit a discussion of the career of Juan Francisco Manzano, the Cuban slave-poet. Besides a number of odes, sonnets, and other lyric poems, Manzano has left us his autobiography, which is a very remarkable document. Here we have the lot of the slave depicted by one who was born to that sad estate. However sympathetic such presentations as Harriet Beecher Stowe's and Whittier's might be, they can never move us as do the pages of this autobiography that are the outpourings of a soul in anguish. We do not wonder that friends of Manzano's masters destroyed the second part of the work, which is a scorching indictment of the patrician family of slave-holders.

A few lines will suffice to illustrate the stark realism of the book. Manzano recalls how once as a child, when he was accompanying his mistress in her garden, he inadvertently plucked a geranium leaf. The consequences he describes as follows:

They took me to the torture chamber, a room formerly used as a sick ward for men . . . but at that time vacant and otherwise unused. The stocks were there and dead bodies were often deposited there prior to interment in the village. My feet were placed in the stocks; the cold was chilling to me as I had no cover. They locked the door. What a night I spent there, lonely soul that I was!

Tragic as these lines are they pale before the story of Gabriel de la Concepción Valdés, who under the nom de plume of Plácido wrote lyrics of a high order of artistry. Illegitimate son of a colored barber and Spanish dancer, Plácido was abandoned in infancy to the mercies of a foundling asylum. His education was meager, but the spontaneity of his muse compensated in part for the discipline of formal studies. His gift for improvisation was remarkable, and he wandered over the island reciting and composing occasional verses in the manner of a medieval troubadour. Unable to support himself and his wife with the scant income thus gained, he established himself in Havana as a maker of combs.

His was a free soul and his love of freedom, together with the envy his gifts aroused, cost him his life. A poem addressed to Isabel Second of Spain contained a veiled attack on Spanish autocracy, and the young poet was imprisoned. On his release, he was more discreet, and expressed his love of liberty by writing a sonnet to William Tell and another lamenting the partition of Poland. Decidedly he was persona non grata to the masters of the island, and in 1844, when an alleged conspiracy of the blacks against the whites was brought to light, he was speedily denounced and summarily condemned to die. Tradition has it that as he walked to his death he recited his famous "Plegaria a Dios," or "Prayer to God," which he had composed in prison. In this poem he protests his innocence and commends himself to God with Christian resignation.

A few words now in conclusion. We have seen what inspiration can come to the Negro as he looks back over the past of Spanish culture. What has the present to offer and what is the promise of the future? If the American Negro looks southward, he will be encouraged and inspired by the spectacle of a similarly despised and disadvantaged people striving toward the same goal of self-realization. Let no one think that the Indian has vanished from the American continent — that his glory ended with the vandalism of Cortez and Pizarro. To the contrary, the indigenous element is strong in Latin America, and the Mexican, the Peruvian boasts that he is more Indian than Spanish. His face flushes with anger and indignation before the spoliation of his splendid civilization by the greedy foreigner, and he is determined that there shall be a renaissance of that civilization. What is the art of Diego Ribera if not a denunciation of the exploitation the Indian has suffered at the hands of state and church, and a promise that the peon will shake off all shackles of physical and spiritual slavery.

The Peruvian poet José Santos Chocano writes "I am the indigenous and savage bard of America." And in tribute to his Indian heritage he sings: "Oh race firm as the tree / that does not bend before the hurricane!"

We, too, know the force of the hurricane, but like the Indian we must not bend. We are engaged in an enterprise that we must pursue with steadfastness, for fair is the prize and the hope great.

JOHN F. MATHEUS

African Footprints in Hispanic-American Literature

Negro slavery was introduced into the oversea colonies of the Spanish Empire ten years after Columbus made his startling discovery. The Portuguese were the traders in this black cargo, until the British, in 1713, obtained a monopoly for supplying the slave markets of the West Indies and the northern viceroyalties and captaincies-general of the imperial rulers of Spain. The influence of the Roman Catholic Church and the weaker virus of colorphobia among the Latin races made it possible for the Negro slave more easily to obtain his freedom and assume something of the status of a free citizen. While he was treated in many instances with such fierce cruelty that Las Casas, the benefactor of the Indians, bitterly regretted advocating the substitution of Negro for Indian slavery, once given his freedom, the black man was not so circumscribed as was, for instance, the free Negro in South Carolina. A fine regiment of black troops was the pride of Havana, for example, during the early days. The proportion of Negro population was much higher, too, in Cuba. The first census of Cuba made in 1774 under the direction of the governor, the Marqués de la Torre, showed the following distribution of 172,620 inhabitants: 96,440 whites, 31,847 free Negroes, 44,333 Negro slaves.[1]

The heroic part played by Negroes everywhere in South America during the wars waged by Bolívar and San Martín for independence and later in Cuba, where Antonio Maceo became a national hero, give abundant reason for pride. Under Spain, too, the Negro proved his valor and

From the *Journal of Negro History*, 23, No. 3 (July, 1938), pp. 265–289. Copyright 1938 by The Association for the Study of Negro Life and History, Inc. Reprinted by permission of the author, the ASALH and the *Journal of Negro History*.

loyalty. Pantaleón Rivarola, Argentine poet (1754-1821), sings the gallantry of two Negroes during the English attempt to take Buenos Aires in 1806. They appear in the poet's "Romance de la Defensa," included in Dr. Henry Alfred Holmes's anthology. Written in ballad form, the verses recount the heroic courage of Pablo Jiménez, slave, who single-handedly had killed two English soldiers in order to rescue his endangered brother. The valiant Pablo, having seriously wounded a third Britisher, carried him on his shoulders to the Spanish hospital in an endeavor to save his life. For these brave deeds the slave was highly praised by his master and by the public and granted his freedom.

Pablo Jiménez and his unnamed companion were not the first to color the pages of new world verse. In the early days, contemporary with the conquistadores, the Negro appeared, even as did Black Stephen, the Moor, Estévanico, who wandered with the shipwrecked Spanish sailor Cabeza de Vaca and led Coronado in a vain attempt to find the golden Seven Cities of Cibola. Alonso de Ercilla y Zúñiga (1533-1594), friend and companion of Philip II, came in the army of adventurers to fight the Indians of Peru and Chile and remained long enough to receive inspiration to write La Araucana, an heroic poem of thirty-seven cantos and some 2,700 octavas. It ranks very high in Chile, where it is considered the national epic, but in other centers arouses less enthusiasm. Our interest in this colossal canvas of war and courageous struggle is the picture the author gives of the Negro selected by the Spaniards to execute Caupolicán, intrepid chief of the invincible Araucanian Indians, glorified by Ercilla along with Lautaro as the real hero of the poem, in depreciation of the Spanish leaders, against whom he was infuriated.

As the story is told in the poem, after the death of the Spanish leader Pedro de Valdivia, Caupolicán was captured by his ruthless enemies and condemned to die. Loaded with chains he was marched to suffer cruel execution by being impaled on a sharp stake. The noble red man's self control is without tremor until he suddenly discovers his executioner is a Negro slave. He asks:

> How? What? Christians, men to honor bound,
> Do you against me, a man of haughty race,
> Plan this thing never in warfare found
> To bring me death at hands so low and base?

The brave Caupolicán then proceeded to go on with his own execution, sat down on the sharpened stake and stoically endured the torture.

Between this scene depicted by Ercilla y Zúñiga and the encomiums of Pantaleón Rivarola had occurred a tremendous reversal in the attitude toward the Negro. Further interesting and revealing insight into the position of the Negro in early gaucho days in the Argentine abound in José Hernández's masterpiece, *Martín Fierro*, that epic of the stretching pampas and the fierce gaucho, taciturn creature of the silent plains.

This epic of an era in the history of the Argentine forever vanished before the march of scientific progress, is composed of two parts, "The Departure," numbering thirteen cantos of 2,316 lines, and "The Return," numbering thirty-three cantos of 4,894 lines. The first part, published in 1872, tells of the terrible wrong perpetrated against the gaucho, Martín Fierro, by the corrupt government. He was conscripted to fight the Indians, and his service was extended to three years by fraud. Deserting, he returns to find that his wife has gone with another man and his sons have disappeared. In fury and despair he crosses over to the Indians to wage war against society.

One of the principal episodes is Martín Fierro's encounter with a Negro couple at a dance hall. Drunken and seeking a fight, he picks a quarrel with the Negro man and his black dancing partner. Insulting the woman with gross remarks, the gaucho tops his abuse in the ridiculing lines —

> God made the whites;
> Saint Peter made mulattoes;
> The devil made the blacks
> To feed hell fire.

In the fierce fight that follows, vividly described, Fierro finally stabs the Negro with the deadly *facon*, or gaucho knife, and the Negro woman with eyes like *ají*, hot pepper, begins to "howl like a she wolf."

"I wished to give her a drubbing," says Fierro, "to see if I could make her keep quiet, but upon reflection and out of respect for the dead man I did not beat her."

The Negro is rolled in a cowhide and buried without benefit of clergy.

> They say that from that time
> When the night is free from rain,
> One can see an evil light
> Of a soul that flees in pain.

Years later, returning again to his long unvisited home, Fierro finds his sons and to two of them relates his sufferings, but the law has forgotten his murder of the *moreno*. Yet he tries to excuse his crime by arguing self-defense, that the Negro cut him first and in the face, "which is a very serious matter," and "if he had been a bit slower, he would have been dead."

Again in a gaucho tavern amidst a crowd of rough and ready fighters, another Negro appears, armed with the race's keenest weapons, song and a guitar. Here the editor pauses to remind us in a footnote that "song and the guitar enkindle the imagination of the Negro." This fact was well known to Cervantes, for in his *El Celoso Extremeño* he tells how a jealous husband left his young wife under seven keys and the guard of the faithful Negro, Luis. The gallant lover comes and in the sweet songs and music of the guitar bewitches the Negro guard so that he opens the door to the rascal. A Negro accordion player, according to the record left by General Mansilla of the Argentine, was a veritable "Orpheus of the pampas."

So Fierro is challenged to a second duel, the *payada,* or contest in improvising verses of song to the slow and monotonous chords of a strummed guitar. This type of musical joust, as old as early Spain and the troubadours of Italy and Provence, was the gaucho's favorite pastime. With a sense of approaching drama silence fell upon the crowd and the Negro began his plaint.

> Very loving is the Negro
> Although he boasts not of it;
> None equal him in affection
> Nor in tenderness of goodwill,
> Like the maca is he
> Who rears his babes beneath his wing.
>
>   *   *   *
>
> Under the blackest face
> There is thought and life;
> Let the peaceful people listen
> And not make me reproach:
> The night, too, is black
> And it has stars that shine.

The *payada* now follows its traditional rules. Martín Fierro asks the Negro six questions, one after the other, as was the right of the person challenged. The challenger answers the six questions one at a time as they are flung at him. The interrogations are, what is the song of the sky, of the land, of the sea, of the night and where is love and what is the law. The Negro responds:

> They say of my color
> God made primeval man;
> But the arrogant whites,
> The same who incited it,
> Forget even to mention it
> And only call my color black.

The white man paints the devil black
The black man paints him white
.Whether the face be white or dark
Argues neither pro nor con:
The Creator did not make
Two classes distinct of men.

The editor notes here that *Lazarillo de Tormes,* the well-known picaresque novel, relates that the widowed mother of Lazarus married a black man and had a son by him. When the mulatto half-brother of Lazarus first saw his father "the child was looking at my mother and at me, both of us white, and at him, who was not, and fleeing from fear to my mother, he pointed with his finger and said, 'Mama, bogey man'." Superstition of the La Plata river section held that when the Indian medicine men conjured up the Evil One he came in the form of a *negrito.* Reference is made also to Marcus Garvey's renunciation of a white God and the substitution of a black Deity and a black heaven.

One more episode will conclude reference to the Negro in *Martín Fierro.* In Canto 21, Picadía, the son of Cruz, Fierro's dead friend and companion, comes to the city of Santa Fé, where he finds some very religious aunts who take him in. There a mulatto girl, a servant in the house, crosses his path. Picardía finds himself unable to remember his prayers unless he thinks of her. The mulatto's presence, he believes, has bewitched him; and she has, but not by necromancy.

Negro characters appear in the two most widely read novels of South America, José Mármol's *Amalia* and Jorge Isaacs's *María,* books which have transcended national boundaries and have become a part of Hispanic-American and even of peninsular literary tradition. *Amalia* presents a vivid picture of the Argentine in the grip of the aristocratic gaucho dictator, Juan Manuel de Rosas. During the course of a twenty-five-year dictatorship, Rosas's tyranny forced many of the progressive youth and liberals of the country to emigrate. To offset this the dictator decreed that death would be the punishment for any citizens caught in an attempt to flee the country. It is this despotic order which supplies background for the love plot between Eduardo Belgrano and Amalia Sáenz de Olobarrieta upon which the author has constructed a tableau of the times. Eduardo and his friend Daniel and others try to escape. Soldiers of Rosas overtake them. In the fight which ensues Eduardo is seriously wounded. Daniel hides him in the house of his cousin, Amalia. The wounded liberal and Amalia become enamoured. All goes well until Rosas gets word that Eduardo is in hiding. The sister-in-law of Rosas, the "Restaurador de las Leyes," with the help of her mulatto servant woman, brings about the detection of Eduardo as a "deserter," resulting in the tragic murder of the youth and his friends.

The nondescript atmosphere surrounding Rosas includes Negroes and mulattoes. "There were gathered and intermingled Negro and mulatto, Indian and white, the lowest class and the middle class, the knave and the good citizen, torn between various passions, habits, prejudices and hopes." Among the classified lists of citizens, *clasificaciones,* drawn up by Rosas in 1835, as for or against his rule, Federalists or Unitarists, an actual historical document inserted in the later editions after Mármol's return from exile, where he wrote his great work, appear the names of Negroes. A significant paragraph begins: "With respect to Negroes of the lowest class, more than nine-tenths of them can be considered as Federalists ready to sustain the cause."

María, an idyllic gem, an immortal love story, of the same genre as Prevost's *Manon Lescaut,* Bernardin de Saint Pierre's *Paul et Virginie* and Chateaubriand's *Atala,* strikes a responsive chord in the romantic Latin temperament. Incidental to the main theme of this melancholy tale is the picture given of slavery in early nineteenth-century Colombia. In the household of Efraín, the unfortunate lover, slavery is presented as a patriarchal institution. As a child he was lulled to sleep by the marvelous accounts of old Peter, the slave.

"The slaves, well dressed and happy as much as it is possible to be in servitude, were submissive and affectionate toward their master.

"My father, without ceasing to be master, maintained an affectionate relation with his slaves, showed a zealous interest in the good conduct of their wives and caressed their children."

The marriage of the slaves Bruno and Remigia is described with interesting details, including the ever-present drums and dancing. The master, to show his good will, condescends to dance a few steps with the modest bride. Juan Angel, the *negrito,* was more companion than slave. It was Lorenzo, a mulatto, who hurried Efraín on his hectic journey from London to his home in the Colombian valley of La Cauca to arrive too late at the bedside of his dying María.

"Lorenzo," I exclaimed, on recognizing a beloved friend in the handsome mulatto who was coming on foot in the center of the custom house.

And precipitously climbing the ship's ladder he clasped me in his arms.

. . . Lorenzo was not a slave. Faithful companion of my father in the frequent trips which he made during his commercial life, all the family loved him and he enjoyed in the house the rights of a majordomo and the considerations of a friend.

. . . His features and appearance showed his energy and frank character. Tall and robust, he had a wide forehead with hair down the temples, a straight and sensitive nose, beautiful teeth, an affectionate smile and a determined chin.

In *Tránsito,* by don Luis Segundo de Silvestre (1886), Colombia has found likewise, a second compelling love romance in the course of which is described the *bunde,* a popular Negro dance.

In the early eighteenth century "El Negrito Poeta," José Vasconelos, born of African Congo parents at Almolonga, Mexico, wrote verses and thus prepared the way for the entrance of the Negro as a contributor as well as a subject in Hispanic-American literature. His verses won tremendous popularity among the masses and were long printed on the calendars of the land of the Aztecs.

"The Mulatto of Córdoba" became a legend in colonial Mexico. Tradition said that a beautiful woman of Negro blood made a compact with Satan himself and thus incurred the wrath of the Inquisition. Just how she was brought before that awful body has been cleverly related in the collaboration of Vicente Riva Palacio and Juan de Dios Peza in a collection of Mexican legends in verse, first published in 1884 under the title *Tradiciones y Leyendas Mexicanas.*

Don Martín de Ocaña, mayor of the village where lived this beautiful mulatto, although well along in years and covered with white hair, became smitten with such a fierce and consuming passion for the mulatto that he confessed his love and showered gifts, tears, pledges, pleading in vain, for his suit was disdainfully denied. Then it dawned upon the aged man that such fixation as his must be more than natural. So he called in the *santo oficio* and had the lady incarcerated in a dungeon. One night a crowd bent on no good intent, led by Señor Ocaña, made its way to her prison.

A gentleman on a fiery steed in great haste passed the mob and in the midst of smoke and flame carried off the charming mulatto. The bold don Martín gave chase, but could not overtake them. The lady, however, did return to the city and was duly condemned to be burned at the stake. One night while waiting for the time of her execution to arrive she was startled by a visit from an aging judge of the Inquisition, who begged the prisoner to save her life by fleeing with him to bestow upon him the gifts of love. Upon her abrupt refusal the doddering judge menaced her with cruel death.

"A minute," said the mulatto. "On the wall is a painted ship which seems about to set sail. What does it lack? Tell me and I am yours."

"Only motion," said the old man after long scrutiny.

"Not even that," laughed the merry witch of color.

She advanced to the wall and as the pictured sea began to roll up waves, stepped aboard the magic ship and disappeared amidst guffaws of diabolic laughter, leaving the wall as before.

The Negro looms large in the folklore of Santo Domingo, as he does of course in her history. Was not Ulises Heureaux, dictator of dictators, a

Negro? Tulio M. Cestero gives his portrait in *La sangre* (1913). An example of the folklore type is seen in this derisive *copla*,[2]

> Look at little Conga,
> She's some colored baby,
> Watch her strut without a flaw
> Pretending she's a lady,
> Ha, ha, ha!

In her introduction to *Florencio Sánchez and the Argentine Theatre,* Dr. Ruth Richardson,[3] summarizing the works of Mariano Bosch and Ricardo Rojas, independent historians of the early Argentinian stage, narrates that the first theatre built in 1781 by the enlightened viceroy Véritz was called *Casa de Comedias,* or *Teatro de la Ranchería,* because of its location, the site of the Negro slave market, *la Ranchería.* In this playhouse the first rows of benches were reserved for the *pura raza,* a special section was set aside for Negroes, mulattoes and soldiers. Mestizos also were restricted.

In Venezuela, country of the great liberator Simón Bolívar, Fermín Zoro (1807-1865), imitating Hugo and Chateaubriand, initiated the Romantic novel. In *La Sibila de los Andes,* "The Sibyl of the Andes," the author takes his theme from Solomon's "Song of Songs," *Negra soi, pero hermosa, hijas de Jerusalén* (I am black, but comely, O daughters of Jerusalem). Elvira, an aged negress, tells of her youth spent with her mistress, Teresa. Reared with her as a playmate, she fell in love with the youth who married her mistress. She pours forth her lament in characteristic *mal du siècle* soliloquy.

Eduardo Blance (born 1838), in the national romantic novel *Zárate,* named for an idealized bandit, makes a Negro, "The Swallow," the outlaw's indispensable henchman. In *Nannelote* a faithful slave kills his wife rather than permit her to betray their master to the Spaniards.

Tomás Michelena in "Three Drops of Blood in Three Centuries," published in Caracas in 1890, presents "The Unknown," the spirit of future Venezuela, whose lineage goes through nine generations of Indians, Negroes and Spaniards to the conquistador Ojeda.

In the short story "La Negra," Rafael Bolívar tells of a faithful slave who chose to care for her penniless mistress rather than to be free. Luis Manuel Urbaneja Archelpohl gives us in "Don Luis" a superman who quells a rebellion of Negro slaves singlehanded; and in "Lo que se derrumba," the decadence of a family, impoverished by sudden freeing of slaves. The granddaughter allows the grandson of former slaves to make love to her.

Manuel Díaz Rodríguez (1868-1927), in his nine stories of color,

Cuentos de color (1898), which appeared originally in the review *El Cojo Ilustrado,* Caracas (following the vogue established by Rubén Darío's *Azul* [1888] and that weird French genius Arthur Rimbaud, in "A noir, E blanc, I rouge, U vert, O bleu, voyelles" [1893], a fetish among the Modernistas), tells in "Cuento gris," "The Gray Story" of Paula, an aged mulatto mother of three sons, whom she lost one after the other, who ended her life in madness.

In "The Sheep and Roses of Father Serafín," from *Peregrino o el pozo,* a novel of Caracas published in Madrid, 1922, a Negro accused of witchcraft is lynched in spite of Father Serafín's effort to save him. The priest goes insane.

Carlos Paz García in 1919 published in Caracas a collection of stories, *La daga de oro.* One of these, "Blanco y negro," relates how Colombine and Pierrot make love, with the change that when Pierrot unmasks he is discovered to be black. In the same author's "Story of the Future" the yellow peril has come and conquered. Paris is the capital of the Mongolian world-empire. But the Asiatics have aped the whites so that they are unable to restrain the African hordes, who, hating the whites, are not corrupted as the yellows. They, too, capture Paris and, finding in the Louvre the Venus de Milo, paint her black.

The most widely known writer among the women of Venezuela is Señora Teresa de la Parra, who won first prize in a novelist contest in Paris, 1924, with her novel *Ifigenia,* which has a Negro laundress among its characters. In *Las Memorias de Mamá Blanca* (Paris, 1929) this sympathetic artist has sketched a delightful picture of country life in the land named for Venice. Negroes are among the most important characters. In a large family of girls, the person who controlled and molded them was Evelyn, the English-speaking mulatto matron from Trinidad, "whose three-quarters of white blood cursed her one-quarter of black blood." She was employed to speak English to her little charges, but delighted them with her article-less Spanish.

Then there was Vicente, the old colored coachman, nicknamed by the children *Cochocho,* the Louse, a loveable character representing the traditional resignation of the Negro. "His soul knew no hate. Being almost of the vegetable kingdom, he accepted without complaining the iniquities of men and the injustices of nature. Buried in the ditch or fixed on the flagstones, whether he was upbraided or not, like a good vegetable he kept on giving impassably his fruits and his flowers." Vicente had the incorrigible habit of coloring the monotony of his dull existence with participation in the interminable "revolutions." Word came to the father of the family that his faithful servant, Vicente, was about to embark again on one of his wild excursions. The employer offered to double his salary and give him a plot of land for his own with a straw-thatchea cabin, but Vicente replied, "I have given my word to the general [Yo le ha dado mi palabra al General]. It was he who made me captain many years ago. I have never worn a pair of shoes, but I am not ungrateful. I will not turn my back upon a protector."

And with a "Good-by, my little girls" on his lips and "May God guard you, may the Virgin preserve you all," he went away, never to come back alive.

The candy vendor, too, is another clear picture. With her white basket and her enigmatic black face, she was, in the wonder-finding eyes of the children, the same as a goddess or a fairy.

This naive mood of childhood has been tenderly sketched by Hugo Wast, pen name of Gustavo Martínez Zuviría, writer of the best-sellers of the Argentine, in his first novel *Alegre*. Alegre was the poetical name given by a kindly white man to a little Negro lad born in Africa on the coast of the Gulf of Guinea. He had been carried off by Arab slave traders and sold away from his parents, landing after many adventures in Buenos Aires. The story moves with the simple abandon of childhood's whims until Alegre finds himself alone before the bier of the little girl he loved and who loved him. Then he leaves his foster home and goes forth to sail the seas as a mariner. In a killing storm he sacrifices his place in the lifeboat to save his benefactor for his motherless children.

In Cuba, where African slavery was not abolished definitely until 1886, the Negro has figured in romantic and realistic portrayals of the cruelties and inhumanities of the system. The first novel of the Cuban poet Gertrudis Gómez de Avellaneda, entitled *Sab*, has a theme similar to Hugo's *Bug Jargal*, published in 1818, which she may have known. As an appeal for abolition of slavery it anticipates *Uncle Tom's Cabin* by some eleven years, although far inferior to Mrs. Stowe's widely read story. The love of Sab for Carlota transcended terrestrial planes. The author makes us shudder at the stupid society which crucified Sab, a great soul, because his skin was tinted, but lauded and pushed to success the heartless and unprincipled Enrique, a cad, so unworthy of Carlota's love that he lacked even the decency to dissemble his mercenary marriage with her.

The 1880 edition of Anselmo Suárez y Romero's Cuban novel *Francisco* contains an advertisement of a one-act play in verse by D. V. Tejero, entitled *The Death of Plácido*. The foreword to the edition of *Francisco* published in Havana, July 23, 1875, when the author was an old man, states his utter inability to make corrections without destroying the verisimilitude of his youthful feeling when he first penned the work whose action took place before 1838.

The real merit of the book lies in the realistic picture of life among the slaves of the sugar plantation, the living hell of the *trapiche* and the perpetual sombre despair of the *batey*, where the heat of the sun scorched by day and the blaze of the fire under the sugar boilers suffocated by night. Contemporary with this and the most outstanding work of this genre is *Cecilia Valdés* by Cirilo Villaverde, an overwhelming tragedy, for Cecilia is the mulatto daughter of a rich slave trader, whose son, Leonardo, falls in love with his half-sister, not knowing the relationship. When he marries a woman of his class, Cecilia urges her mulatto lover, Pimenta, to attack Leonardo and kill him, as the infuriated Hermione goaded Oreste to assassinate Pyrrhus in Racine's *Andromaque*. And always present is the fascinating background of the Havana of the 1830s.

Felix Solom continues the Havana background tradition in depicting the contemporary metropolis of the island republic through the tinseled life of *Mersé*, a colored girl. Yet none of these novels has a stronger note than the love of Francisco for Dorotea, forever thwarted by the lecherous son of their mistress, who lusted for the beautiful slave girl, a compelling motif running through the pages filled with sorrows, *llorando a mares*.

José A. Fernández de Castro, in an article in the *Revista Bimestre Cubana*, gives a picture of the Cuban Negro in Cuban Letters.[4] Something of the importance of Plácido, Gabriel de la Concepción Valdés, may be measured by the fact that Dr. Coester devoted six pages to him in his *Literary History of Spanish America*.

Turning our attention now to the present scene we find a great recrudescence of interest in the Negro all over Latin America. Dr. Carter G. Woodson has pioneered in the whole cult of bringing before civilization the long-buried relics of the Negro in the old and the new world. Not always because of high literary merit but that it may be made known that the Negro has not been mute, inarticulate. The words of the Mexican peon's melancholy song apply to the Negro:

> I sing that they may hear my plaint,
> Not for the sweetness of my song,
> I sing that they may hear my groans
> At home and all the world along.[5]

From Montevideo, Uruguay, came in 1929 Ildefonso Pereda Valdés's *Raza Negra*, a book of Negro poems and African and Afro-Montevidean songs. From Cuba by way of Spain arrived in 1935 Emilio Ballagas's *Anthology of Hispanic-American Negro Poetry*. This volume contains poems on Negro themes by seventeen poets, four of whom are of Negro origin, Marcelino Arozarena, Regino Pedroso, Ignacio Villa and Nicolás Guillén, whose *Motivos de son* have been set to music by the contemporary Cuban composer Amadeo Roldán.

To the English reader of Spanish the strikingly unique feature of many of the poems in the latter collection is the marvelous rythmic effects reproducing the pulsations of the African dances, the wild and hypnotic vibrations of the *rumba,* the *habanera,* the *bunde.* A translator may well nigh despair of reproducing the effects of the sonorous Spanish consonants and singing vowels, especially in the original onomatopoeic creations, beating in perfect measures the music of the drums. For example, in José Zacarías Tallet's *La Rumba* –

Zumba, mamá, la rumba y tambó,
mabimba, mabamba, mabomba y bombó.

Then follow the rush of the dancers' feet and the rattle of the gourds filled with pebbles –

Cháqui, cháqui, cháqui, charáqui.
Cháqui, cháqui, cháqui, charáqui.

Vachel Lindsay gained something of this effect in his *Congo,* but his art is a bit more sophisticated.

Now must the curtain fall. The panorama of the Negro in the letters of Latin America is gorgeous with all the rich, lush and lavish colors of the tropics, with the warm, pulsating beat of that dark stream of blood. Latin America, both Hispanic and Portuguese, cannot be expressed without the pigment of the tinted races, the Indian and the Negro.

NOTES

1. Vidal Morales y Morales, *Nociones de Historia de Cuba* (Havana: Libreria "La Moderna Poesía," 1906), p. 120.
2. Julio Arzeno, *Del Folk-Lore Musical Dominicano* (Santo Domingo, R.D.: Roques Roman Hermanos).
3. New York: Instituto de las Españas en los Estados Unidos, 1933.
4. "El aporte negro en las letras de Cuba en el siglo XIX," *RBC,* XXXVIII, No. 1 (July-August, 1936).
5. Atl, *Los artes populares en México,* II (Mexico City: Editorial Cultura), p. 109.

ANTONIO OLLIZ BOYD

The Concept of Black Awareness as a Thematic Approach in Latin American Literature

Black awareness as a method of interpreting the literature of North America and the Caribbean is an accepted and uncontested approach.[1] Concomitantly, black writers in the English-speaking areas of this hemisphere have raised their literary voices to express an esthetic reaction to society's cultural dictates of a black/white dichotomy. Lemuel A. Johnson, in *The Devil, the Gargoyle and the Buffoon: The Negro as Metaphor in Western Literature,* has found a most applicable quote by Lewis Nkosi that, in part, explains the intent of the black esthetic: "Black consciousness really begins with the shock of discovery that one is not only black but is also non-white."

However, Latin American writers, of both Spanish and Portuguese expression, have yet to be added to this corpus of ethnic critics in numbers comparable to those of the northern hemisphere. And whenever there is black awareness as a thematic approach in the literature of Latin America,[2] Nicolás Guillén seems to be the sole object of literary criticism. Initially, we might conjecture that this is due principally to the difference in standards of ethnic identification for the two areas, English-speaking versus Spanish- and Portuguese-speaking. Latin Americans, in general, have an almost nebulous approach when overtly ascribing labels of ethnic identification. To explain to someone who is outside of the culture exactly what is intended by such racial epithets as *negro, negrito, morena, mulato, mestiço, trigueño, caboclo,* etc.,[3] becomes confusing when one tries to associate the phenotype with the genotype. Nonetheless, whatever the ascription, there is inherent in the lexicon of Spanish and Portuguese a psychological orientation of non-whiteness that runs the gamut of color gradation. This leads us to consider whether or not there exists for non-white Latin American writers a perspective of ethnically oriented race awareness based on a concept of color, and whether we are justified in placing the burden of this artistic perception on the aging shoulders of Nicolás Guillén. To reconsider our conjecture of Latin American ambiguity in the ascription of racial categories, we find that even Guillén exposes the duplicity that is implicit in this tendency. In his "El abuelo," the attack on this hypocritical stance is quite overt:

> This angelic woman of northern eyes
> who lives attuned to the rhythm of her European blood,
> does not know that in the depths of that rhythm a Black man
> beats the hard drumhead of wild drums.
> . . . . .
> Oh, my lady. Look at your mysterious veins;
> . . . . .
> for you will see, restless near the cool bank,
> the soft dark shadow of your grandfather who flees,
> the one who permanently crinkled your golden hair.

Consequently, while most critics of Latin American literature refuse to acknowledge non-whiteness as an esthetic concept, given the mere numerical presence of blacks and near-blacks in most Spanish- and Portuguese-speaking areas of the hemisphere, and their participation in the literary arts, surely a psychological recognition of in-group versus out-group behavior patterns must be present in the Gestalt structuring of their themes. Consider the fact that Guillén (the acknowledged exponent of black awareness) not only attacks the infectious habit of pretending to be white, but reverses the alleged pattern of miscegenation. Those Latin Americans categorized as *mestiço* or *mulato, trigueño, pardo,* etc., are unvacillatingly considered to be the product of an illicit, at times licit, union of a white male and a black female. (In this paper, we have not considered Indian and Indian-white esthetics, since such an all-inclusive approach would have to be extended to weigh the genetic hierarchy of Black/Indian societal acceptance.) The discerning critic, however, notes that Guillén has placed the onus of miscegenation on a black male/white female relationship, cognizant that such a union is taboo in traditional occidental literature. True, there have been attempts by non-black authors such as Rómulo Gallegos in *Pobre negro* to show that there are in Latin America descendants of white female/black male unions, but such authors view these relationships negatively. In their novels, the aura that surrounds such sexual unions is replete with acts of violence, and the relationship functions to the moral, psychological and/or sociological detriment of the black male participant. Guillén, while overtly denigrating "pureza de sangre," reverses the pattern of racial mixture, and metaphorically approves the union: "La dulce sombra oscura del abuelo que huye" ("the soft dark shadow of the grand-father who flees").

While not all Latin Americans openly reject black progenitors, they require a different orientation to accept the reality of their social situation. This is evident in the concept of black awareness as a thematic approach; a case in point is Rubén Darío, the initiator of the modernist movement in Hispanic letters. Darío belittles the possibility that a drop of African or Indian blood runs in his veins, and when he uses the black theme, he is insensitive to the subtleties that guide the esthetic concept of a black awareness. While visiting the Cuban poet, Julián del Casal, in Havana, Darío was inspired by local black beauties to write the following:

> Do you know Black Dominga?
> She's an off-shoot of Kaffir and Mandingo,
> she's an ebony flower filled with sun.
> She loves ochre and red and green,
> and she has in her kissing, biting mouth
> a thirst for the Spanish kiss.
>
> Serpentine, fiery and violent,
> with salt and pepper caresses
> she trembles and reveals her wild passion:
> she has a fire that Venus praises
> and the Queen of Sheba would desire
> for the bed of King Solomon.
>
> Conqueror, magnificent and wild,
> with the cunning of a cat or panther
> she extends her feverish embrace to the white man
> and in her mouth, where a kiss goes mad,
> she reveals teeth of coconut meat
> with reflexions of milky marble.

Offensive to the concept of black awareness are the ethnic stereotypes of the black woman who is so often portrayed in Western literature as "serpentine, fiery and violent, with salt and pepper caresses." She is often a sex object or a symbol of primitivism, and she yearns for sexual union with the white male. Frequently, she is a caricature, revealing "teeth of coconut meat with reflexions of milky marble," combining black skin and exceedingly white teeth. The blond golden-haired princesses of Darío's modernism are treated with more respect and dignity. Respect, dignity and truthfulness to the preconceived self, are, in the main, the dictates of the black psyche as racial awareness develops in South America. For example, Gaspar Octavio Hernández (1893-1918), a black Panamanian modernist, is exemplary of the tendency:

You will see neither pearl-colored skin,
nor golden hair adorning my face with finery;
nor will you see sapphire light,
heavenly and pure, stored up in my pupils.

With burnished skin of the swarthy Moor;
with dark eyes of fatal blackness,
I was born on the Bay in the dark green
foothills, facing the sonorous Pacific.[4]

Here, one sees recognition of self, acceptance of self, and pride in self. Consequently, the esthetics of Hernández are perceived and understood as a part of the self-image even in verses where he sings of the black woman:

Sweet brown woman, brown woman
stained by the chicken coop,
when you go out, the slums
smell of roses and jasmine.

In addition to the ambiguous question of racial identity in Latin America, there is also the erroneous impression that slavery in Latin America and slavery in the United States were different. Consequently the United States was more susceptible to rhetorical militancy and the struggle for liberation. Hortensia Ruíz del Vizo, in the introduction to her anthology *Black Poetry of the Americas,* states:

Slavery in colonial Spanish America was not as harsh as the same institution in English America. . . . Several influences, however, mitigated the harshness of the institution. One of these was the influence of the Catholic Church. . . . In the United States, the history of the black population, as we know, has been different. . . . Nowhere as in the United States does the black live a more painful existence. . . . The *black spiritual* may be seen as the offspring of this suffering. . . . The actual existence of the spiritual shows the difference between the Spanish and the United States bondage. The spirituals are, in fact, unknown in the Spanish countries. There, instead, the black music is full of happiness and merriment.[5]

Such a statement ignores the creative suffering that Juan Francisco Manzano (1797–1854) experienced in colonial Cuba:

For thirty years I have known the world
for thirty years I have lived in pain
and sad misfortune attacks me on every side;

but the harsh battle that I have waged
in vain is nothing to me
if I compare it, oh God, to what lies ahead.

Manzano, a self-taught slave, seems to have been so affected by the political execution of his black compatriot, Plácido, that he put an abrupt end to his literary career. Both he and Plácido were suspected of participating in a slave insurrection. This experience and his sensitivity to the plight of Cuban blacks evidently caused him to abort his literary career. While the blues or spiritual atmosphere is evident in Manzano's verses, there is none of the "happiness and merriment" that del Vizo perceives. There is nothing optimistic about Manzano's poetry; on the contrary, a romantic pessimism pervades the poetic ambience of these verses. The poet has spent thirty years of painful existence in this world, with sad misfortune assaulting him from all around; however the foregoing battle that he's withstood is nothing compared with what lies ahead. "Oh God!" is his desperate plea. Of such intensity is black spiritualism when set to music.

In this writer's opinion, the underlying phenomenon of black awareness is that it transcends techniques, and surfaces again and again as a thematic approach. Actually, black awareness tends to fill in the thin space that exists between technique and theme to emerge as an entity of esthetic method. Percy Lubbock, in *The Craft of Fiction: Picture, Drama, and Point of View,* finds that method is shaped by point of view. Point of view, for him, is the relation in which the narrator stands to his story. The poets who are cited above have used poetry as a critical axis of reference, illustrating that point of view is a dramatic force in poetry. The negative point of view of Manzano is an esthetic expression of his faltering hope for the future, as a black man. However, a novel which illustrates the importance of point of view is *Juego de dominó* (Game of Dominoes) by Manuel Mora Serrano,[6] a Dominican writer. Without a doubt, the major theme of this *novelita* is political, but the technique is introspective as the characters reveal their thoughts in monologues and "stream of consciousness." Nonetheless, the author's presence is felt; he constantly focuses our attention on a character's thoughts, and the final summation of the novel is obviously his. However, in spite of the control that Mora Serrano exercises over the thought and movement of his characters, the characters are functional. They are representative of the socio-ethnic atmosphere, and give the political theme coherence. There are few descriptions of characters in *Juego de dominó,* but the reader receives the distinct impression that the characters are black. There is only one possible reference to a white person, and it is ambiguous; the reference is either to a white person or the blank space of a domino. On the other hand, there are several references to blacks (italics below are mine):

he let his eyes fall without malice on the robust arms of *that mulatto creole* as if he were looking at the national flag.

Fausto Rey was a hit, and you could hear his soft *black creole* voice . . .

I see him tall and agile, slender and *brown* like a dear oak.

and my eyes moved greedily over the strong *brown thighs* . . .

Color gradations are referred to as:

One woman with her long, thick hair and *light color,* and the other *dark,* with her cute tricks . . .

her distant eyes . . . in her *dark face* . . .

I see the *dark skin,* the sharp nose and tight lips . . .

I saw those *pale* faces . . .

Although politics takes precedence over race as the leit-motif of *Juego de dominó,* it is evident that the ethnic ambience is thematically constructed by someone who finds no need to denigrate blacks or to portray them as exotic and primitive. One senses that they represent the ethnic majority, and that they are a projection of the author himself. Wellek and Warren suggest in the *Theory of Literature* that "these problems of social origins, allegiance, and ideology will, if systematized, lead to a sociology of the writer as a type, or as a type at a particular time and place." Mora Serrano subtly reflects black awareness in his writing. In a letter dated March 11, 1974, the author informs this writer:

Last year, we held our first international meeting at the University of Santo Domingo on African culture; this is an indication of the great over-sight which we, in these areas, have historically shown toward Mother Africa, out of an ardent desire of Hispanic identification. Although there is linguistic logic for this, it is unjust given the fact that 95 per cent of us are mulattoes. Even though some of us cherish the blackness that we carry within, one senses a certain apathy for identifying as such. Without such an identification we are hardly half of a country.[7]

This statement is evidence not only of the author's sociology but of the inherent sociology which one perceives in *Juego de dominó.*

The sociology of the author can also lead to a transcendental black-ness, as in the case of Joaquín Beleño C., a black Panamanian novelist. His novels revolve around the peripatetic existence of the Panamanian in the Canal Zone who is an unwanted, ill-treated stranger on his own soil. His novels seem to project a personal reaction to real situations. For example, *Gamboa Road Gang* (1960) is based on the trial of a black Panamanian who was accused of raping a white North American girl. Although some have described the Panamanian populace as an amalgam of blacks, whites, and Indians Beleño decries a black/white Panama. One wonders if his social origin, allegiance and ideology have raised the level of his black consciousness. His *Curundú* (1963) is the story of a Panamanian student who goes to the Canal Zone to work during the summer vacation. Economics and not race is the main issue of this novel; however, the protagonist, Rubén Galván, views his world within a racial perspective. His enemy is described as white, blond, red-necked and prejudiced, the North American "gringo." The Panamanian counterpart to the "gringo" is also described:

"I can go any place where there are gringos. I am as white as they are, and even whiter. . . . Furthermore, I am from the most aristocratic family of Panama."
"So what? It's all the same to the gringos; to them you're all 'spiks.' You are blond, but here everyone is mixed with blacks. . . ."
"In my family no one has had anything to do with a Negro. Never!" exclaimed Fulo Alejandro, about to become indignant. Fani restrained his voice when he answered; but he observed:
"Here even the blonds look like Negroes or become half black."

While "el Fulo Alejandro" is the ally of the "gringo" who exploits him, the protagonist, Rubén Galván, functions effectively in a racially chaotic world. The "gringo" sees Rubén as "brown," and Rubén prefers this classification to black:

It must be incomprehensible to a Saxon that a Latin should make a distinction between black and brown, as Rubén Galván seems to do. . . .

In reality, he would have enjoyed being white:

When he took part in those activities, Rubén Galván considered himself white, and not just white, but he also failed to understand and comprehend why he wasn't blond with blue eyes; . . . neither could he believe that he was a half-breed who was browner than he really deserved to be. . . .

His perception of self is inextricably related to his racial identity. White American women are irresistible sex objects, although he understands that they are taboo. Rubén feels a close bond with the black West Indian immigrant because both the black Panamanian and West Indian are socially rejected by the "gringo." It is through such innuendoes that the author alludes to a racism based on color and economic factors. The subjectivity of Beleño's intimations reveals the black perspective of the author just as the characters in Mora Serrano's *Juego de dominó* reflect the author's rejection of the institutionalized invisibility of the black man. Conceptually, is this black awareness? In spite of the theory that racism does not exist in Latin America the fact of the matter is that one is white or non-white. The various terms in Spanish or Portuguese that describe degrees of whiteness or blackness become factors in a built-in escape system. Such terms are a way of expunging a psychological blot through lexical maneuvering, since the artist's reaction to his society is in large measure interpreted psycholinguistically. To accomplish this he relies on covert symbols or an overt lexicon. And where race is a thematic factor either intentionally or unintentionally, the discerning reader captures through language alone the mental attitude of the author's stance on race.

B. D. Amis, in his Ph.D. dissertation, *The Negro in the Colombian Novel,* concludes that the treatment of blacks in several works seems to depend in large measure on the author's attitude toward blacks, although black awareness as a theme is not his primary concern:

I have singled out for examination the theme of the Negro in the prose fiction of Colombia because many Colombian authors have chosen to assign a broad and significant role to the black man in their works. . . . The primary focus of this study will be to examine novels of literary merit and show how they depict the Negro artistically. Thus, the literary craftsmanship of the author will be analyzed together with the apparent theme, intent and inevitable social content of each novel.

As stated, his intent is to examine literary movements, such as romanticism, *costumbrismo,* realism and naturalism, and themes such as social protest to determine how the black character is developed. Since each movement has its own themes, techniques and esthetic, the black character is important only insofar as he projects the concerns of the author. Amis determines at the conclusion of his study that, in the main, white novelists gained fame in their literary portrayal of the black Colombian because they adhered to the social mores of their period. However, black authors such as Arnaldo Palacios and Manuel Zapata Olivella presented the black as an existential being, probed the black psyche, and attempted a sentient portrayal of the black character. Palacios wrote within the confines of naturalism, while Zapata Olivella wrote novels of social protest.

In the critical approach to black Latin American literature, one must determine if there is black consciousness, and if this consciousness produces thematic verisimilitude. Such verisimilitude involves psychic and physical visibility from a black point of view, and must be considered as a secondary theme if the primary theme is not racial. Where race is the primary theme, the black writer must make his characters credible. When the ethnic composition of Latin American society is reflected in literature, race becomes a major theme, as we have seen in the works of Darío,

Guillén, Hernández, Beleño and others. The author's point of view thus shapes and controls his material. Black awareness, for Latin American authors, is a thematic contour which is psycholinguistically controlled by race relations in the area. Black awareness seems to be a vital theme amongst the non-white writers of Latin America. To accept this truistic concept enables us to provide the proper perspective for its thematic position in the literature. It is this position that will undoubtedly help us to uncover the corpus of true black writers in Latin American literature.

NOTES

1. Refer to such articles as "The Negritude Tradition in Literature" by B. M. Wright and "Thematic Patterns in Baldwin's Essays" by Eugenia Collier, or the Introduction to *Caribbean Rhythms,* ed. James T. Livingston (New York: Washington Square Press, 1974), p. 7.
2. Richard A. Preto-Rodas, *Negritude as a Theme in the Poetry of the Portuguese-Speaking World* (Gainesville, Florida: University of Florida Press, 1970), p. 77. This author presents us with an approach which might be considered prototypical.
3. Charles Wagley, *An Introduction to Brazil,* rev. ed. (New York: Columbia University Press, 1971), p. 122. Here Wagley lists the myriad terms in Portuguese that try to adjust phenotype to genotype classification. See also Kal Wagenheim, *Clemente* (New York: Praeger Publishers, 1973), pp. 36–37, and his *Puerto Rico: A Profile* (New York: Praeger Publishers, 1972), pp. 16–17, 157–159, an observation of the confusing pattern of genotypical/phenotypical nomenclature which is prototypical of Latin American race consciousness.
4. Rodrigo Miró, *La literatura panameña* (San José, Costa Rica: Imprenta Trejos Hermanos, 1972), p. 209.
5. Hortensia Ruíz del Vizo, *Black Poetry of the Americas: A Bilingual Anthology* (Miami: Ediciones Universal, 1972), pp. 9, 15, 16.
6. Santo Domingo: Ediciones de Taller, 1973.
7. I have translated Mora Serrano's comments to me, in answer to a question regarding black awareness in present-day literary trends in the Dominican Republic which I posed in a previous letter.

ADALBERTO ORTIZ

Negritude in Latin American Culture

Ethnographic studies of Latin American countries, and particularly of Ecuador, traditionally treat only two racial groups – the autochthonous Indian and the conquering white race, frequently slighting the anthropological importance of the black man who completes the racial mixture. We are all aware of the virtues and the vices or defects of the white cultures which subjugated the indigenous peoples, crushing or deforming their civilizations. Fortunately, in the last few decades there has been increased interest in and a scientific systematization of archeological studies; these studies have led to surprising discoveries in regard to the American cultural past.

The contribution of black people, however, has hardly been studied. Although blacks were forcibly brought to this continent, under cruel and inhuman circumstances, they were able to transport much of their African culture, and to impose various elements of their art and religion on many regions of the New World.

Tales and Legends

African tales have been preserved in America because of their utilitarian function. In a way, they compensated for slavery; in stories about animals, for example, the most astute always triumphs over the strongest or the meanest. In this regard, there is the story of Uncle Tiger and Brer Rabbit, in which the latter always makes fun of the former, and

Translated by the editor from "La Negritud en la cultura latinoamericana," *Expresiones Culturales del Ecuador,* 1 (June, 1972), 10-18.

the story of the Trashman of the mountain (the anteater), a clever animal who fights his enemies by mimicking them.

In the United States, the famous stories of Uncle Remus have been preserved with some authenticity, and in Brazil Monero Lobato and other authors have collected many tales of African folklore. These tales were preserved orally by the Mammies, Black nannies, nursemaids or *mae preta* [Black grannies], who told stories about black people to white children in order to entertain and teach them. These stories were then translated into the diverse languages of America by educated whites.

It is also interesting to note the transferal to this continent of many jungle creatures — creatures such as the *Tunda* of Esmeraldas and the *Patica* of Colombia, who, like the Bantu *Quimbungo,* frighten children to make them obey their parents or to prevent them from wetting their beds or going out at night and wandering into the jungle. Another of these supernatural creatures is the Mother of Water, who lives in the mouth of the river and who has a counterpart in other regions of America heavily populated by blacks.

In the Caribbean, especially in Haiti and Jamaica, we have the stories of Bouki, Jean Saute and Malice, who outwits the dimwitted Bouki. No one can miss the symbolic significance of these creatures whose struggle represents the silent animosity of slave and master. In Jamaica, the stories of "Miss Nancy," or of the spider Anancy in the African language, are famous. It would take too long to list the stories, folk tales and legends that have been brought to America, but these are the major factors which have significantly influenced Afro-American culture and what we now call "Negritude" on our continent.

Concepts about Negritude

It is obvious that just as people have spoken about Christianity, Spanishness, Latinity, Slavery, etc., we can justly speak of Negritude, with all its ups and downs. Negritude, or Blackness, is viewed as a cultural and literary doctrine that was born in America, or, rather, in the Caribbean, where the black population lived in closer contact with both the African and the European culture. The word was first coined by the great Martinican poet Aimé Césaire within the poetic context of a "return to the native land" or to Africa. This movement spread to all areas where people of this race live. Spanish-speaking black writers rapidly spread this great cultural movement. In passing, I must state that, in my opinion, Negritude is only a means of expression and affirmation, and not an end in itself, as extremist theoreticians-politicians of this movement propose; their position would lead us to an anti-racist racism, to a sort of black Nazism. Basically, the theory of Blackness is no more than the result of frustration, but it can develop into an expressive generosity based on almost forgotten cultural traditions. Negritude, in Africa and, later, in America, has always been subjected to and oppressed by white culture; it has been dominated by unconscious forces. But it was able to survive and to manifest great strength in the nineteenth and twentieth centuries, when erotic dances were refined and introduced into elegant salons. Negritude, then, has a solid sociological and, more importantly, philosophic base.

Negritude seems to be an effective and logical antithesis to the humiliating universal insult that the white man has inflicted on the black in the last four centuries. Negritude or Blackness rejects the past, to the extent that the past incorporates slavery and alienation. Negritude had to oppose white contempt with a justifiable arrogance. It responded to decadent European reason with rebellious and violent literature: to gawdy ceremony and stiff protocol with liberty, candor and exuberance; and to blind imitation of an exhausted European culture with an unconditional affirmation of the once-forgotten African culture. Exaltation of Negritude opposes, above all, the generalized acceptance of a supposed black inferiority.

At any rate, Negritude is not a passing phenomenon, because it has reestablished for us the legitimacy of belonging to an African culture, as well as to the Hispano-European and Indo-American cultures. In this way Negritude has been converted into a definite profession of faith, a spiritual attitude, and a liberation from decadent forms. Its spontaneity constitutes a manifestation of an almost sexual joy in nature. It is a good incitement to live in reaction to long suffering and misfortune. But, in less dogmatic terms, Negritude for Americans cannot now be a "return to Africa," or an exaggerated defense of African culture, but, rather, a process of ethnic and cultural miscegenation on this continent that can be powerfully appreciated in these times not only in the physical manifestations of inter-marriage, but also in the esthetic ramifications of a particular literary movement, as well as in folk music, beliefs and superstitions.

Historical and Social Antecedents of Negritude in Ecuador

From the depths of Africa, a painful echo that was also joyful and militant resounded through the Esmeraldian jungle until just a few years ago; it was the sound of primitive musical instruments, the laughter of carefree blacks, and the clinking of fierce machetes, which were often used to sever heads as well as to farm. Black men experienced pain and misery, servitude and abandon, but beneath everything, they always had a latent desire for liberation and fight. It might be well to point out, in passing, that slavery was not established in the province of Esmeraldas, as it was, most harshly, in other American regions, because the area was settled by escaped slaves. According to the chronicler of the Indies, M. Cabello Balboa, around 1553 a Spanish galley bound for Peru with a cargo of seventeen black men and seven black women ran aground on the coast of Atacmaes. The Spanish crew decided to lower the slaves to the ground, where they escaped into the dense jungle and, in this way, obtained their freedom. Later, these fugitive slaves took over the whole region, sometimes with peaceful methods and sometimes with violence. Their first chief was Antón, who was succeeded by the famous Alonso de Illescas (raised in Seville), who established a real dynasty and created serious political problems for the Spanish Crown, because the territory that he controlled extended from Manabi, Ecuador, in the north to Buenaventura in Colombia. (In the seventeenth century, similar events occurred in some areas of the Caribbean when English or French slave ships ran aground.)

The influx of slaves and fugitives from Colombia increased the population of that region, and these blacks greatly influenced the folklore, customs and dialectal forms of Ecuador. It appears that the black Esmeraldians, the product of intermittent secondary migrations, were primarily of Dahomey, Yoruba and Bantu origin, as one can deduce from some words and utensils used in that region of our country. Because of the diversity of the cultures, African survivals are weak and difficult to determine with precision; however, in Haiti or Cuba, where the majority of the Africans were from Dahomey and Yoruba, respectively, African religions such as Voodoo and the syncretized *Santería* were established. Black Esmeraldians played a major role in the political wars of the end of the last century, according to the account of the historian Roberto Andrade. In the famous Alfarist campaign of Colonel Carlos Concha, his integrated troops, composed for the most part of colored people, kept the government army in check for four years. Because of this civil war, the province fell into economic ruin, the fields were devastated and abandoned, and the starving population emigrated. Cattle raising and agriculture, once flourishing, practically disappeared. The only thing left was the happy and carefree spirit of the inhabitants. The province made a slight comeback between 1920 and 1930, with economic cycles in the development of natural resources such as ivory nut, vegetable marble, and rubber, which was plentiful in the forests. The exigencies of the Second World War created a great demand for balsa wood. Ironically, the abundant natural resources of the region has been prejudicial, in some ways, to its progress, because the peasant, who does not have to work hard to harvest the fruits and woods that grow naturally, has had no incentive — until very recently — to develop agriculture. It is only in the cultivation and exportation of bananas or cotton that farmers have had to work with systematic regularity; however, in recent years development of these crops has also suffered an alarming decadence and deterioration.

In Esmeraldas, the black man added a distinctive and appealing folkloric note to the Ecuadorian shore with the primitive syncopated music of the marimba, bass drums, bongo drums, guasas and scrapers, music that could be adapted to happy celebrations, or could be used for funeral wakes by those who sang the Song of Praise and the Moonlight songs. The life of the colored Ecuadorian was spent hunting, fishing, or working on the banana plantations and cattle ranges; sometimes he worked independently as a timber raiser, and very rarely he worked in a light industry. The women took up domestic work and spent Saturdays and Sundays in the dance halls, where they forgot the long hours of work, dancing and drinking beer or brandy with men. Because of various economic, migratory and sociological factors brought on by integration, Esmeraldas is fast disappearing and changing into the depersonalized face that is the result of progress.

Before continuing, it is necessary to point out the presence of a minority black group that lives in the hot valley of Chota, a province of Imbabura; these blacks were brought to Ecuador from Colombia by Jesuit priests to cultivate sugar cane. They have preserved customs, music and folklore which are characteristically Afroid.

During my infancy and adolescence, my spirit was nurtured by the Esmeraldian atmosphere. I began to see, hear and feel. I had personal experiences that, years later, would develop in me "that great confusion" that Goethe defines as literature. The literature written by blacks and mulattoes of the twentieth century has been so distinct that it has earned the black man a separate chapter in universal literature, entitled "Negritude."

Negrist poetry began in Golden Age Spain with the humorous and interesting, although superficial, works of Góngora and Lope de Vega; later, it appeared in Mexico with Sor. Juana Inés de la Cruz. However, it is only in the second half of the nineteenth century that a true precursor of this poetry emerges in the person of the black Colombian, Candelario Obeso, although some of his compositions have a purely romantic touch (a romanticism that led him to suicide), as befits the period. But the major work of this literature, including Afro-Castilian poetry, short stories and novels which treat social and racial problems in original styles and distinctive forms, has only reached fruition in our time, that is to say, since blacks have become racially conscious and have gained an awareness of their own creative worth. Before, they felt that they had to imitate; now, on the other hand, their cultural and artistic forms are imitated and studied. They exert a powerful influence on the productions of occidental nations, especially in music and the plastic arts. It is worth pointing out that "Negritude" poets and artists have not only what is called "inspiration," but they also have something profound to tell and to say, because black poetry is primarily functional and, therefore, is incompatible with surrealism. Nevertheless, African arts are much more diverse than the people of other races imagine; these arts exhibit a variety of modalities that carry them beyond realism or idealism and outside of the traditional Euro-American classifications. Finally, our literature is perhaps a type of expressionism in which words create images, and not the contrary, as in the European lyric. African or Afro-American poetry generally has a theme, motifs, and content which are reinforced by rhythms and sounds that penetrate the body until it reaches, in some cases, a cosmic-visionary extasis.

Insofar as Ecuador is concerned, the movement appeared a bit late. The anonymous black poets of Esmeraldas sang folk *décimas* in which they mixed Christian saints with Spanish historical figures. Country folk narrated symbolic animal tales (like that of Uncle Tiger and Brer Rabbit, for example), stories of brave men and incredible ghosts, and tales with a moral or picaresque content; most of these were of African origin. It was only at the end of the Thirties that the poet and novelist Nelson Estupiñán Bass and I began to write Negrist poetry, novels and short stories in the Caribbean manner, using, however, our own elements and materials to give our work a national flavor. Beginning in the Forties, we wrote novels and some short stories with the black theme. Estupiñán has written some black novels, such as *Cuando los Guayacanes Florecían (When the Guaiacum Bloomed)*, which takes place during Carlos Concha's civil war; *El Paraíso (Paradise); El Negro y el Río (The Black Man and the River);* and several books of poetry: *Timarán y Cuabú,* which contains folkloric *décimas; Huellas digitales (Fingertips),* etc. Years later, other young writers emerged, the most notable of whom is the poet Antonio Preciado, with his beautiful book *Tal como somos (Such as We Are).* It won the national poetry prize of the newspaper *El Universo de Guayaquil.* His poetry, not always typically Negrist, has great lyric value. Presently, the young poet Orlando Tenorio has great promise, as has the black actor and reciter Washington Caicedo, who writes sonorous Negroid poems with a humorous and rebellious tone. There are other Ecuadorian writers of different generations and from other provinces who have written picturesque or anecdotal short stories and poetry with Negroid themes rather sporadically and superficially.

My (Negrist) Literature

Since I am a mixture of blacks and whites, my literary personality is more oriented toward a dichotomy, so that at times I write works which are black in content and in form; at other times I treat themes of racial mixture; and I sometimes write literature that could be signed by white men.

When I wrote poems in the Negrist mode, I found that a particular style was needed, a style that included onomatopoeia and especially the phonetics used by the black masses of my country. It is known and understood that deformed Spanish, English and French are not spoken by blacks because they are black, but because they have not had access to educational institutions. I have also noticed that in the Spanish and African languages, and in Creole or patois, Negrist poetry acquired its greatest drum-like sonority, and not in English or French. To obtain musical effects in such poetry, another ingredient was necessary: the syncopated and monotonous rhythm of primitive music, music that is vernacular and folkloric. These effects can be achieved by placing the nasals n and m in front of consonants, and by using, at the end of lines, words which terminate with a final accented vowel. Such words convey the sounds of percussive instruments. In addition, I also use foreign words of African extraction, adding a new contribution to national semantics. I did not forget, of course, the most pronounced characteristic of black art, that which gives it its typical and imperative dramatism, the anaphora, or repetition of notes of musical phrases, of words or phonemes, and of decorative flourishes. I did not forget the intuitive or collective nature of this type of art. There exists in Negrist poetry a polyrhythm, rhythmic counterpoints that strip the verbal rhythm of a regularity that could become monotonous. It is like a mathematical formula that is based on unity within plurality, with secondary forms and rhythms, with phonemes and sounds that reinforce the magical efficacy of the whole. The poet of African ancestry never subjectively uses his individuality as a theme; rather, he uses nature and manipulates it to create a new form of life: Kuntu [the form or modality].

The anaphora and its variants — reduplication, epanadiplosis, conduplication — convey to him a sort of magnetic enchantment and mystic, ecstatic and sensual raptures. This poetry also uses paronymous alliterations. Like other Negritude poets, I soon discovered that formal decoration, *bembosidades*, as the Hispano-Cuban sociologist and essayist Fernando Ortiz called them, and *jitanjáfora* were no more than skin and form; it was necessary to penetrate deeper to the social human core, because my poems were more dance than song in the beginning. I became aware that Negritude is not only a matter of style, but also of content.

The first poem that I wrote was "Jolgorio" ("Frolic"), and I continued writing until I had finished a book of black motifs. Because it was impossible to publish it in Ecuador — for during that period the Casa de la Cultura Ecuatoriana [an Ecuadorian publishing house] did not exist — I had to wait until 1945 to publish it in Mexico, with the title *Tierra, son y tambor (Land, Sound and Drum).*

Almost at the same time that I composed these poems, I began to write, in Guayaquil and Milagro, my novel *Juyungo: historia de un negro, una isla y otros negros (Juyungo: Story of a Negro, an Island and Other Negroes)* to enter in a national contest. This type of black novel has similarities with Victor Hugo's novel *Bug Jargal,* which takes place during the time of Haiti's slave insurrections. It also is like the novels of the African Thomas Mofolo, or those of another precursor of Negritude, René Maran, a Martinican official in the Colonial Service in Africa who won the Goncourt prize with his novel *Batuala.* In the United States we find several black writers who are not exactly Africanists, such as Langston Hughes, Richard Wright and, finally, James Baldwin. These writers, particularly Richard Wright with his novel *Native Son,* which has few, if any, African elements, have a universal range. In Latin America, there also appeared novels with African themes and customs such as *Rey negro (Black King),* by the Brazilian Coelho Neto; *Jubiaba* and *Mar Morto (Dead Sea),* subtitled *Yemayá,* novels by Jorge Amado; *Pobre negro (Wretched Negro)* by the Venezuelan Romulo Gallegas; *Rizaralda,* by the Colombian Bernardo Arias Trujillo, and *Ecué Yamba O,* in Cuba, by the Franco-Cuban Alejo Carpentier.

Juyungo deals with the life, from puberty to youth, of a black peasant who dies uselessly in a war. It is the drama of a primitive and wild man who tries to penetrate and understand, in an elemental way, the world in which he happens to live. It is a problem of conflicts between blacks, whites and Indians; it is a case of discovery and identification, that goes from racial hatred to class struggle, from social problems to the fight against injustice. Since it is a work in prose, about black, social, racial and cultural themes, seasoned with folkloric and costumbrist elements, I thought that it would be best to find a style suited to its content, that is to say, to convey, in prose, the rhythm and musicality of Negrist poetry, with a style similar to that which I used in poetry. I believe I have achieved balance, for the most part, especially in the inscriptions "eyes and ears of the jungle." Unfortunately, this form is lost when the book is translated into other languages.

On several occasions, I have also written short tales which employ the black theme, as in the case of the story "La entundada" ("The Girl Who Was Bewitched by the Tunda"), "La mala espalda o los contrabandistas" ("Evil Fate or the Smugglers"), "Los amores de Fernand Muret"

("The Loves of Fernand Muret"), etc.

Since this paper has the sole purpose of interpreting, a posteriori, the phenomenon of Ecuadorian Negrist literature, particularly mine, in relation to Negritude, whose esthetic and philosophic influence has come in part from unconscious sources, I will not analyze my other literary works, which are classifiable as manifestations of what we could call white, western literature.[1]

NOTES

1. In a letter to the editor, Adalberto Ortiz acknowledges his indebtedness to the following sources: Janheinz Jahn, *Muntu;* Ndavaningi Sithole, *El rito de Africa;* Frantz Fanon, *Condenados de la tierra;* Georges Bolandier, *Africa ambigua;* Roger Bastide, *Las Américas negras.*

SHIRLEY M. JACKSON

Fact from Fiction:
Another Look at Slavery in
Three Spanish-American Novels

There is a wealth of information about slavery in Spanish American literature, including two novels, *Cecilia Valdés* By Cirilo Villaverde and *Sab*
by Gertrudis de Avellaneda, and the short story "Nay" intercalated in the
novel *María* by Jorge Isaacs. All of the authors write about the experiences
of men and women of African ancestry in the New World. In addition,
however, the novels present narrative material rich in the literary tradition
of romanticism, but, more importantly, these selections present precise
and detailed accounts of events which occurred in Spanish America near
the end of the slave period.

The aim of this study is, through a brief summary of these novels,
to reveal to an English-speaking public a dimension of slavery which is
often overlooked and which, hopefully, will also stimulate research on
African influence in Hispanic civilization. Historians, social scientists and
students of language and literature will discover much about slavery — and
the institutions and laws which fostered its rampant growth — in the
grim accounts of atrocities described in these works.

For example, the Cuban judicial system, with its "sliding scale"
of justice, denied "legitimacy" to Cecilia Valdés when her European father
refused to acknowledge the mulatto woman's paternity. The father,
Señor Gamboa, migrated to the New World from Spain to improve his
economic situation; as an advantaged white man, he believed that "los
negros" were animals, no different from *un tercio* of tobacco. Don Can-
dido Gamboa explains to his wife, Doña Rosa, an aristocratic Havana
socialite that

when the world is convinced that Blacks are animals and not men, then
one of the motives that the English cite to discourage the African trade

83

will be finished. A similar thing is happening in Spain with tobacco. . . . Do you think tobacco has a soul? You better believe that there's no difference between a *tercio* of tobacco and a Negro, at least in so far as the ability to feel is concerned.[1]

Another feature of colonial mentality during the slave period is revealed in the philosophies and doctrines of Church and State. For example, the Church purported to transform savages into spiritual beings, as Luis M. Díaz Soler, the Puerto Rican historian notes:

[The Church believed that] it was transforming a savage, a heretic, into an individual capable of enjoying the pleasures of western civilization. The man whom God created free was enslaved in the name of civilization and progress.[2]

Evidence to the contrary is present in the centennial edition of *María* in which the story of "Nay" appears. In a very detailed study of the novel, the noted South American editor Mario Carvajal comments that slavery was profitable to all, and that in many instances the Church abnegated its responsibility by refusing to condemn slavery or criticize slave holders. Carvajal traced Church apathy to the Vatican in Rome and the laws promulgated by Pope Pius II after 1492. For corroboration of these facts, Carvajal recommends the book, *Historia universal de Cantú*, especially Chapter 6. A study by Marvin Harris, an anthropologist and author of the essay "The Myth of the Friendly Slave Master," refutes the belief which was prevalent in nineteenth-century South America that slavery was beneficent and enjoyable to the enslaved.[3] This myth is evident in the novel *María* when the son of a slave owner observes to his father:

The slaves, well dressed and as happy as it was possible to be in servitude, were submissive and affectionate with their master.

Marvin Harris maintains that many owners would have been left with barren fields had their slaves been given the opportunity to return to Africa, although a few slave owners admitted, however reluctantly, that slavery was unjust. Harris also points out that each slave owner was convinced that his slaves fared better than any others, although it was difficult to find witnesses to refute the theory that slaves were content. He notes:

The testimony of the travelers, poets, planters, abolitionists, and scholars in this matter, however, is worthless. Better to dispute the number of angels on a pinhead than to argue that one country's slavery is superior to another's. The slaves, wherever they were, didn't like it; they killed themselves and they killed their masters; over and over again they risked being torn apart by hounds and the most despicable tortures in order to escape the life to which they were condemned.

There were laws to protect slaves, but these were not effective, because the attitudes and values of the Spanish planters prevailed, especially in the back country, where the great landowners' word was law.

Much can be learned from the customs of a people, and the New World of the nineteenth century was colored by a variety of singular traditions. For instance, it was customary in most Spanish American communities for the master and his sons to visit the slave compound during religious festivals and other celebrations, which served as the only social outlets for slaves. These holidays were often used as training sessions for the sons, who learned how to control the Black masses and prevent uprisings.

Efraín, the protagonist of *María,* and his father attend a slave wedding celebration, extend the usual greetings to the group, and then join the festivities. Efraín's father even dances with Remigia, the Black bride, and such intermingling of the races accords prestige to the ceremony, while at the same time it affords the white males an opportunity for future sexual exploitation of slave women.

Similar customs prevailed and relationships existed between whites and freed slaves; Cirilo Villaverde contends, for example, that white clergymen and slave owners often "graced" festivals in the "barrio negro." Such ceremonies became known in Cuban urban society as "frijoles con arroz" (beans with rice), a term which alluded metaphorically to the mixture of the races. Indeed, it is at one such festival that Leonardo Gamboa, a frivolous and wealthy white man, first sees the beautiful mulatto, Cecilia Valdés, whom he intends to exploit sexually. For Cecilia and other freed slaves, life in the Americas provided a kind of pseudo-freedom, but their more advantaged social status afforded little improvement in their psychological and socio-economic problems. As Ernest Lewald contends:

during the Colonial Period, the social pyramid reserved the lowest levels to the Indian peasant and the African slave; and just a little higher up were the half-breeds and mulattoes.[4]

Sab, the Cuban protagonist of the novel bearing his name, is a fair-skinned mulatto whose only crime in life is to have been born to an African woman. Gertrudis de Avellaneda presents Sab as the ideal slave; he is noble, loyal and handsome, and is so unusual that he is appointed "mayoral," or overseer, of the Bellavista plantation. He performs his

duties well until he falls in love with Carlota, the sensitive daughter of
Sab's white master. Carlota has always admired and respected Sab; they
were playmates during childhood. She regards him as amiable and faithful
— the ideal servant. Because he realizes the futility of his situation, Sab
tries to conceal his love for Carlota through a series of intricately planned
stratagems designed to prevent her marriage to the unworthy Enrique
Otway. This son of an English immigrant merchant is favored by Carlota's
father as a suitor for his virgin daughter. The match is also approved by
Enrique's father, an astute businessman who, having lost most of his
fortune, desires the economic advantages of such a marriage.

Neither Enrique nor his father knows that Bellavista, which in earlier
times was a rich plantation with numerous slaves, has had to reduce its
labor force, primarily because of a series of financial setbacks which forced
the gradual sale of slaves and property. Carlota's father manages to conceal
his financial plight from the Otways, and the marriage takes place.

Sab's characterization evolves as the novel draws to an end. Beset
with grief, Sab is now presented as the sentimental victim of love. Des-
titute and self-pitying, Sab agonizes over his impossible love and his status
as a slave who is regarded as less than a man, a pitiful creature without a
country. One morning he is found dead by a long-time friend, and when
Carlota discovers his death and learns of his love for her, she spends the
remainder of her life seeking religious consolation.

Another view of Spanish life during slavery is presented in the story
of Nay in the novel *María*. In this story, the author underscores the exotic,
as is commonly done in romantic novels. Rather than denouncing the
evils of slavery as did the authors of *Sab* and *Cecilia Valdés,* Isaacs uses
the slave narrative as an artistic or esthetic device. Enrique Anderson
Imbert, the noted Spanish American literary critic, explains:

It was just that exoticism was such a typically romantic feature that Isaacs
could not resist it; and he gave us the story of Nay and Sinar in an African
setting. Africa was for Isaacs what America was for Chateaubriand. Isaacs'
description was not realistic; he saw landscapes with eyes which were
already accustomed to the romantic style. The only pleasure to be derived
from nature was, for him, a romantic arrangement. Isaacs knew, of course,
that landscape was a great literary theme. And he developed it as a state
of mind, in typically romantic fashion.[5]

As he develops his narrative, Jorge Isaacs describes the Chocó region
of Colombia in which the novel *María* takes place, and then describes
"exotic" Africa. Although the author had never visited the African continent, he conjures up a good tale with vivid descriptions and some facts.
Isaacs relates an idyllic love story of Nay, an African princess, and Sinar,

a captive slave warrior, who are cruelly separated by a group of European slave hunters. The story then develops into a highly stylized version of the long and tragic history of the African woman in the diaspora. Nay becomes one of many women who were destined to spend the rest of their lives as captured slaves in the alien and hostile lands of the Americas. For Nay, life on the new soil brings only grief, despair and the realization that she will never return to her beloved homeland. In the New World she is raped by a cruel master and is left alone with a son, Juan Angel. She is further humiliated by being forced to change her name from Nay to Feliciana; although the new name is easier for whites to pronounce, the change of name symbolizes the loss of her last spiritual bond to Africa. After serving several slave masters, Nay realizes that she can never return to Africa, which for her is now only a dream. Nevertheless, it is this image of Africa that becomes her symbol of freedom, as the memory of her homeland spurs her onward in a quest for the liberation of her son. She achieves her final wish on her death bed when her master signs the "papel de manumisión," granting freedom to Juan Angel. The paper of manumission, which grants only conditional freedom, is another of the many barriers to freedom in the New World. The paper grants freedom to Juan Angel on the condition that the boy remain a loyal servant; it does not prevent the daily humiliations that the child must suffer at the hands of his master. While *Sab* depicts a male denied the full measure of his manhood, the story of Nay is a testimony to the dehumanization of a woman and a child.

Another view of slavery in nineteenth-century Spanish America is presented in *Cecilia Valdés o la loma del Angel.* Cecilia Valdés is the name of the central character in the novel and "la loma del Angel" refers to Angel mountain, the ghetto of Cuban mulattoes. Unlike the other two novelists, Villaverde undertakes in his work the colossal task of describing Cuban urban society. By projecting vignettes of Caribbean life onto a series of "cuadros" or paintings, Villaverde reveals the customs and attitudes of colonial times. Cecilia Valdés, the protagonist, unifies the novel and binds disparate selections into a single view of urban society. Cecilia is a free descendant of slaves, and she represents the beautiful mulatto woman who is locked into an environment which provides no outlet for those who refuse to be exploited. The name "Valdés" was given to Cecilia and to all other mixed children whose fathers refused to recognize them; her plight was shared by many other children whose sexually exploited mothers were abandoned by their lovers.

The heroine, struggling for respect and psychologically conditioned by the attitudes and institutions of the time, deludes herself that she is superior to others of African descent because of her white blood. Although she is loved and respected by José Pimienta, a darker mulatto, she rejects his offer of marriage because such a liaison would adversely affect her social mobility. Success by Cecilia's standards means acceptance (through marriage) by white society. Ironically, however, Cecilia emulates her mother by forming an illicit relationship with the son of her mother's lover, her half brother. Although warned by those of her "barrio," Cecilia encourages Leonardo's advances only to find herself pregnant and abandoned by him later. In her despair rage turns to insanity, and she is eventually committed to a mental institution, where she finds her mother wandering the halls of the "manicomio." In the meantime, the Gamboa family has arranged a socially acceptable marriage for their son, but on the day of the wedding José Pimienta avenges Cecilia's honor by plunging a dagger into Leonardo's chest.

Because all of the characters in these fictional works — Cecilia, Nay and Sab — die tragically, the helpless victims of a cruel system, it might appear that resistance and rebellion were not evident among Black Latin Americans. However, this is not true. Cecilia tries to escape from her untenable situation by striving to attain social acceptability in the white world. Although she is unsuccessful in achieving her goal, José Pimienta, her mulatto suitor, avenges her dishonor by killing Leonardo in an act which symbolically "castrates" the white male. Nay resists through the act of survival; she determines to live in order to free her son, Juan Angel. This same resistance is evident in Sab, who refuses to accept his slave status. Angered by the status which emasculates him and denies him the love of Carlota, he bitterly protests the injustices of Cuban society and heroically tries to save Carlota from a disastrous marriage.

All of these examples attest to the exorbitant price that African people in the diaspora had to pay for freedom. The ability of these people to adapt their lives to stringent circumstances is manifest repeatedly in these works. For instance, in the novel *Cecilia Valdés*, the "cuadros de costumbres" describe the unique ambience of Afro-Cubans who earn their livelihood as musicians, gardeners, tailors and craftsmen. This fictional account of life in the "barrio" is corroborated by Fernández de Castro, who describes the situation of freed slaves and mulattoes during this period in his book *Tema negro en las letras de Cuba*. The ability of New World Africans to adjust to harsh circumstances is also affirmed by the historian John Hope Franklin, who maintains that, in spite of the heterogeneity of the African people, they possessed sufficient common experiences which worked to fashion new customs and traditions in the Americas. The African heritage is preserved in the rich oral tradition reflected in Nay's tales of her homeland, in the music and dance described in the novels, and in the characters' speech patterns, which combine the

African and European languages.

The three novels present a fairly accurate history of an African people in the Americas. Chancellor Williams, the noted historian and author of the brilliant work *The Destruction of Black Civilization,* underscores the fact that in the midst of unparalleled hardships, the strength of African people can be measured by their ability to organize and reshape their lives into meaningful cultural bonds which have been transmitted from generation to generation for centuries. In the past, the continuous division of African peoples into smaller units has led to mass migrations throughout the continent. It is precisely this movement, according to Chancellor Williams, that has given the African people unity and strength as a race.[6]

Like their African counterpart, Africans in the diaspora, especially those in the Americas, have also been unified by the struggle to survive; the three Spanish American novels attest to this. The story of Nay is one of survival which culminates in the promise of a new life for the sons and daughters of Africans. The child that Cecilia Valdés bears represents the hope of those who are destined to forge new lives in the Americas, while the tragic story of Sab is emblematic of the tremendous price that Blacks paid for their freedom in the New World.

NOTES

1. Cirilo Villaverde, *Cecilia Valdés o la loma del Angel* (Havana: Editorial Lex), p. 317.
2. Luis M. Díaz Soler, *Historia de la esclavitud negra en Puerto Rico* (San Juan: Editorial universitaria, 1970), p. 17.
3. *Slavery in the New World* (Englewood Cliffs: Prentice-Hall, 1969), p. 44.
4. *Latino-américa: sus culturas y sociedades* (New York: McGraw-Hill, 1973), p. 239.
5. *Historia de la literatura hispano-americana (la colonia cien años de república)* I (México: Fondo de cultura económica), p. 316.
6. *The Destruction of Black Civilization (Great Issues of a Race from 4500 B.C. to 2000 A.D.)* (Dubuque: Kendall Hunt, 1971), pp. xv–xvi.

LESLIE WILSON

La Poesia Negra: Its Background, Themes and Significance

Black poetry, as we know it today, constitutes a rather recent development in the Spanish-speaking countries. Fifty years ago, most of the Black
poets in different parts of the New World, including the United States,
followed European poetic themes and molds quite faithfully. During the
second decade of the present century, various Spanish-speaking poets from
the Western Hemisphere initiated enormous soul-searching efforts for the
purpose of discovering new poetic forms and inspiration. Ironically enough,
however, the reading of scholarly books on African civilization and culture
written by Europeans was what encouraged Latin Americans to discard
their Europeanized manner of poetic expression in favor of verses that
relied upon African concepts, themes, and rhythms. European scholars
such as Delafosse, Frobenius, and others had discovered in the "primitive"
cultures of Black Africa a captivating music with forceful rhythmic patterns and subtle overtones which they considered somewhat lustful in
nature. Ethnologists, painters, adventurers, and others thronged to Dark
Africa to drink from its bountiful fountain of human knowledge and
artistic inspiration. Many of those who visited the African continent were
seeking a lifestyle devoid of a number of the western world's rigid, and
often meaningless, social obligations.

Sub-Saharan Africa possesses an ancient, but well-preserved, oral
literary tradition in the form of poetry, fables, tales, and myths that
had been almost ignored by outsiders until then. The history of Black
African kingdoms such as Benin, Mali, and Songhay, to mention but a

Translated by Leslie N. Wilson. From "El negro en la poesía hispanoamericana," CLA Journal, 13, No. 4 (June, 1970). Reprinted by permission of
the author and CLA Journal.

few, dates back many centuries. The rediscovery of Africa south of the Sahara brought to the fore a different concept of the plastic arts. This "new" artistic mood was characterized by the distortion of forms and the use of color for emotional expression.

A number of scholars were intent upon gathering abundant data concerning the "exotic" Black Africans who had managed to preserve quite hermetically the ancient rites and ceremonies of their forefathers. Of these scholars, Leo Frobenius (1873-1938), German explorer and sociologist, deserves special mention. In a series of publications, Frobenius revealed some remarkable information regarding scientific and cultural accomplishments of Black Africans. His best known work, *The Black Decameron,* published in 1910 and translated widely, helped to propagate legends, myths and assorted oral literature from the heart of Black Africa.

African sculpture drew admirers in Paris and Berlin. With its bold lines and daring designs, it revolutionized the plastic arts of the western world. Some of Picasso's paintings give evidence of African influence. Two of the faces of *The Damsels from Avignon,* which was painted by Picasso in 1917, are imitations of African ceremonial masks. His painting entitled *The Dancer,* a work forming part of the Walter P. Chrysler, Jr., Collection in Chicago, is actually a reproduction of a Bakota figure from the Congo. Certain works painted by Braque, Derain, Vlaminck, and Matisse were inspired by African works of art. The Fang idols, the Baluba figurines for religious offerings, the Ife masks, the masks of Bapende and Basonge, and the ritual ornaments of Bampara were all imitated in European paintings produced in the early part of this century. The African-inspired mode caused great waves of excitement, both in Europe and America.

The French poet Apollinaire published an album of reproductions of these motifs in 1917. Several years later, Blaise Cendrars published his famous *Black Anthology,* a work that includes abundant data pertaining to cosmogonic legends, fetishism, totemism, and other African cultural tendencies. André Gide journeyed through the Dark Continent and later published an account of his African experiences in *Voyage to the Congo* (1927). Philip Soupault, the French surrealist writer, incurred in the African theme with his poem "The Black Woman" (1929).

At about this time, the African-inspired music known as "jazz" was receiving tremendous ovations in Europe, as well as in America. Louis Mitchell, a Black American, had introduced European audiences to jazz in 1914. Several years later, Jim Europe and the members of the all-Black 369th Infantry Regiment Band were showing Europeans and fellow members of the American Expeditionary Forces in France what a topflight military band could do with jazz music.

Jazz, an important Black contribution to United States culture, had a rather long and interesting incubation period. In the cotton-growing regions of the United States, African rhythms were transmitted from one generation to the next by means of camp-meeting shouts, work songs, and spirituals, which gradually gave rise to the *blues*. Music, for a long time, had served numerous transplanted Africans in the United States as an outlet for frustrations and pent-up emotions. This continued to be the case with the advent of jazz. The idiom of blues and jazz was used as an expression of the Black mood in poetry, in the theater, in the novel, and in light operatic works. In the United States, Black poetry in its purest form was elevated to lofty heights during the 1920s — the period of the Harlem Renaissance — by Langston Hughes, Arna Bontemps, James Corrothers, Claude McKay, Countee Cullen, and other great Black poets. It is interesting to note that during the 1920s, there took place also in Latin America a resurgence of Black poetry. Although the genesis of Black poetry in the Latin American countries is somewhat different from that of Black poetry in the United States, it can be said that Latin American poets received a great deal of assurance and inspiration from the Harlem Renaissance poets.

Dr. Howard M. Jason, in a brilliant and well-documented essay, points out that the Black theme made its appearance in Spanish literature in the oldest known Spanish theatrical work, a liturgical play entitled *Auto de los Reyes Magos (The Magi)* which was written in the twelfth century. The Black theme in Spanish grew in importance until the end of the seventeenth century. At that time, Spanish literature entered into a period of decadence that lasted almost throughout the eighteenth century. Modern Afro-Spanish poetry, in some respects, had its incubation period in works produced by such noted Spanish authors as Bartolomé de Torres Naharro, Luis de Góngora y Argote, Francisco de Quevedo, Simón Aguado, and Lope de Vega, all of whom belong to the Golden Age or the period immediately preceding it.

It should be pointed out here, nevertheless, that most of the African-inspired poetry written before and during the Golden Age of Spanish literature should rightfully be referred to as negroid or pseudo-Black poetry. This is because it fallaciously portrays the Black man from a highly superficial point of view. Its primary objective is that of comicity. Little or no attention is given to the great manifestations of the Black people's soul, their deep emotions and noble sentiments, or even their human dignity. On the other hand, as Angel Valbuena Briones has pointed out, the dances, the linguistic peculiarities, and the stereotyped characteristics of the Black race were used quite skillfully. The *bozal* speech, or the childlike gibberish of the Blacks who had recently arrived from Africa, which was considered as symbolic of the buffoon, was imitated freely in the portrayal of Black characters.

Lope de Vega, realizing the possibilities of the Black theme, included in his vast theatrical repertoire a number of Black men and women, whose buffoonery and witty sayings in broken Spanish provoked great laughter. In *The Virgin's Chaplain (El capellán de la Virgen)*, he introduced the song "Your Grace's Snout" ("El hocico de vosa mercé"), while in *The Unsoiled Cleanliness (La limpieza no manchada)*, he staged, with Christian symbolism, a dance ritual on the killing of a snake: "Of a Snake We Are Thinking . . ." ("De culebra que pensamo . . ."). Góngora contributed to the movement with his "Zambambú, Dark Lady of the Congo . . ." ("Zambambú, morenica del Congo . . ."), from his work entitled *On the Feast of the Holy Sacrament (En la Fiesta del Santísimo Sacramento)*. Quevedo, his rival poet, wrote "Blackfolks' Wedding" ("Boda de negros") — a famous piece of satire.

The treatment of the Black theme by sixteenth- and seventeenth-century Spanish writers is much closer to the modern Afro-Spanish poetic movement than the average layman would expect. At times, the themes are very much alike. The feigned Puerto Rican song that Sor. Juana Inés de la Cruz composed for the vespers held in honor of Saint Peter Nolasco in 1671 compares quite favorably, from the standpoint of rhythm, to Nicolás Guillén's "Black Chant" ("Canto negro").

The following is a stanza from the aforementioned poem by the Mexican nun:

> Tumba, la le, le, le,
> tumba, la, le, le
> que don Pilico escrava
> no quede.
> Tumba, tumba, la, le, le
> tumba, la, la, la.
>
>   * * *
>
> Boom, dah, dey, dey, dey,
> Boom, day, dey, dey,
> for I, Pilico, a slave
> did not stay.
> Boom, boom, day, dey, dey,
> boom, dah, dah, dah . . .

This stanza is from the formidable Afro-Cuban poet's "Canto negro":

> Tamba, tamba, tamba, tamba,
> tamba del negro que tumba;
> tumba del negro, caramba,
> caramba que el negro tumba.

* * *

Bam, bam, bam, bam.
Rhythm for the Black man to get it on down.
The swelling of Black rhythm. Oh, man!
Gosh! Watch that Black dude go to town.

Although there is evidence of marked stylistic improvement in the latter poem, in the former the basic rhythmic elements of the more modern *poesía negra* are present.

The nineteenth century also witnessed the inclusion of certain portions of Black tradition in poems and light theatrical works. A very good example of this is *A Hot Pepper or the Wedding of Pancho Jutía and Canuto Raspadura* (Havana, 1847), a little theatrical work written by Cretó Gangá, which spotlights Black folklore in its comic treatment of theme and characters. "Song of the Absent Vogue" by Candelario Obeso, a Colombian poet, together with his "Farewell, My Dark Lady," are other examples of the Black theme in Spanish American poetic and light theatrical works of the nineteenth century. The Dominican poet Juan Antonio Alix, one of the greatest Latin American popular poets of his time, wrote "Black Behind the Ears," which treats the problems of those who try to "pass."

African slavery in Latin America produced a transculturation phenomenon. Yoruba and Bantu groups had been sent to the Spanish West Indies and the South American mainland. Dahomeyans were sent to Haiti and Louisiana; while the Fantishantis ended up in the British West Indies, British Guiana (now Guyana), and Virginia. These stalwart Black men and women were to help shape the character of neo-Africans in different parts of the New World. The Blacks who inhabited the Spanish colonies sought refuge and protection in clandestine organizations (secret societies) that received the name of *cabildos* (municipal halls) in the Caribbean and *naciones* in the southern part of South America. The *ñáñigos*, the first of the groups to gain renown, originated in Cuba in 1835. In 1914, there were 57 *ñáñigo potencias* (societies) in Havana. These groups held religious ceremonies and dances that were offshoots of African tribal rites and ceremonies. To avoid opposition from the religious hierarchy, they adopted saints of the Catholic church and members of the Holy Family as patrons of their feasts and celebrations, attributing to them fetichistic powers.

As is to be expected, music occupies an important place in Afro-Antillean religious activities. The Cuban musicologist, sociologist and folklorist Fernando Ortiz has pointed out that there are as many different songs as there are phrases present in the very complex Black Cuban ritual.[1]

Since literature has resorted to, and incorporated, these aspects, one should be acquainted, partially at least, with Afro-Caribbean cosmogony. Such knowledge will lead to fuller understanding and appreciation of this art form. Nicolás Guillén, in his "Bongo Song," makes reference to the two counterposed and parallel worlds which underlie the consciousness of many *afrocubanos:*

> Saint Barbara on one side,
> on the other side, Changó.

A primitive concept of Catholicism is blended with African theological concepts. Dark deities share their secret rites with popular Christian saints. Olorún, Lord of the Heavens, who is worshipped in the Caribbean and in Bahía (Brazil), could indicate a monotheistic tendency comparable to that of the Christian God. A series of *orishas* or saints are ambivalently venerated. Obatalá is syncretized with Our Lady of Mercy. Changó, "the God of Thunder," is the "male Saint Barbara." Especially popular with the "initiated" is Ifá, who possesses full knowledge of the secrets of fertility and conception. Among the orishas of lesser category are Ogún, "God of War," who is sometimes confused with Saint Peter; Babayú-Ayé, who is similar to Saint Lazarus; Oshún, comparable to the Virgin of Charity *(la Virgen de la Caridad de Cobre),* and Yemanyá, the Afro-Cuban counterpart of *la Virgen de la Regla.* Eshú, a god with malefic powers, is evoked in the worship of Souls of the Dead.

References to church dignitaries are rather commonplace in Black popular songs in Latin America. The following stanza from a well-known Puerto Rican *plena* bears this out:

> Mommy, the bishop arrived.
> He's in from Rome, by golly!
> If you could only see him, Mommy.
> What a pretty sight! How jolly!

In the *Afro Montevidean Songbook,* edited by Ildefonso Pereda Valdés, we find another interesting example of this in the poem "Francisco Moreno":

> My name is Francisco Moreno,
> and I've been over to confess
> with the parish priest
> who understands my illness.
> *Curembé, Curembé, Curembé.*

At other times, the poet makes mention of a few Black divinities to set the scene. This point is well illustrated in the following fragment of

"Yelidá," an interesting Black poem by the Dominican poet Tomás Hernández Franco:[2]

> This is not the story of Erick, who, finally,
> at the age of thirty, sold herrings from Norway
> at his little store in Fort Liberté,
> while Erick's wife, Madame Suquí,
> to Legbá and Ogún for her white man did pray. . . .

The *cabildo* songs, or *comparsas,* had dramatic plots that were to be enacted and accompanied by dances. Of these plots, the death of the snake was perhaps the one that possessed the greatest folkloric value. The ancient ritual snake dance, performed on Three King's Day (Epiphany), began with the chant

> The snake is dead.
> *Sángala muleque* . . .[3]

The contortions of the singers' bodies conveyed the symbolism of the snake-killing act. The ritual can be referred to as the beginning of a stereotyped art with scenic effects. Guillén's "Sensemayá" constitutes a representative portion of this link with Africa. Another religious festival, the *candombe,* provided the motif used by the Uruguayan artist Pedro Figari in one of his most famous paintings. Pereda Valdés brilliantly adopts the *candombe* as the central theme of one of his Afro-Uruguayan poems. Using the *baquiné*[4] theme, Luis Palés Matos produced one of his foremost Black poems.

Some very interesting and picturesque folklore characters parade through the pages of the *poesía negra.* Among these figures are Baldomero ("Papá") Montero, the cane-swinging, rumba-dancing, carousing *ñáñigo* who was knifed to death by a drinking partner while on a spree; the Negro Bembón with his jiving and "shucking"; José Ramón Cantaliso, sharp-tongued itinerant musician who gets the Yankee *turistas* told, and Mamá Inés. Not to be forgotten is María Belén Chacón, the tragic figure whose lungs felt the bitter bite of tuberculosis as a result of her long nights toiling over a hot iron.

The poesía negra makes use of all the local color and folklore within its reach. However, it refrains from using folklore elements which are not its own. The *mariyandá,* the *baquiné,* the *candombe,* the *bomba,* the *plena,* superstitions, chants for killing snakes, and *ñáñigo* rites are all interpreted in this fascinating literary movement.

The first budding of poesía negra was visible in the Modernist movement. Rubén Darío himself, with a rhetoric which was quite apropos, *mandinga, cafre, ébano, pimienta, marfil,* suggested a propitious environment in "Do You Know Dominga the Black Lady?" ("¿Conoces a la negra Dominga?"). The Panamanian Demetrio Korsi (1899-1957) continued the master poet's example with the creation of the popular figure Chimbambó. Felipe Pichardo Moya (1892-1957), a Cuban poet, anticipated the great Afro-Antillean poetic expression in the Spanish language with "La comparsa," a poem that captures the gaiety and color of carnival festivities.

Luis Palés Matos, an outstanding Puerto Rican poet, initiated the poesía negra movement in 1925 with his poem "Black Town." Aided by Afro-Antillean musical elements, onomatopoeic words, African words, references to places in Africa, rum, sex, Blacks, mulattoes, and various aspects of Afro-Caribbean folklore, the captivating Black theme became fashionable in all social circles.[5]

Palés's poem entitled "The African Dancer," a poem written in 1918, belongs to the superficial category of poetry about Blacks which should rightfully be called negroid or pseudo-Black poetry. The works by Palés's countrymen that are mentioned below, together with countless others by Spanish-speaking poets from other countries, are also *poemas negros de visión exterior,* or pseudo-Black poems. They include "Schoolmaster Ralph," by José Antonio Daubón; "Indiana," by Luis Felipe Dessús; "Joseph the Black," by José Antonio Daubón; and "Black Man and Black Woman," by Luis Lloréns Torres.

From 1928 on, the Black theme has been used by Spanish-speaking poets of Latin America as well as of Spain. Without a doubt, the early interest in the poesía negra was spurred along quite a bit by the anthropological studies of the Cuban scholar Fernando Ortiz, as well as by the Afro-Cuban music vogue which swept the world from the late Twenties through the Fifties.

In 1930, with the publication of Guillén's *Motivos de son,* Cuba became the artistic center of the poesía negra. The list of contemporary poets who have cultivated Black poetry in Spanish is extensive and the themes dealt with are varied. Black poetry made its appearance in all the islands of the Caribbean, circled South America, and ultimately reached Spain. In all of the areas mentioned, it found staunch admirers and erstwhile cultivators. It should be noted that two of the cofounders of the Afro-French movement called *Négritude,* Aimé Césaire and Leon Damas, were born in the New World. The Negritude movement contributed greatly to the achievement of independence in Francophone West Africa. Claude McKay, one of the principal poets of the Harlem Renaissance, was a native of Jamaica.

The high priest of the poesía negra is Nicolás Guillén (Camagüey, Cuba, 1902). The poetry of Guillén begins with popular *costumbrista* motives steeped in the fascinating rhythms of Afro-Cuban melodies. It established a dramatic dialogue with the use of visual images which made his art more profound. This poetry finally became an anguished call for the improvement of the socio-economic conditions of the West Indian islands.[6] Guillén's compatriot Emilio Ballagas (1910-1954) is another member of the great triumvirate of outstanding writers of the poesía negra movement. The third member of the triumvirate is, of course, Luis Palés Matos (1898-1957). Guillén is a mulatto, while Ballagas and Palés Matos were white.

The art of Luis Palés Matos manifests his great literary knowledge and ability, as well as his superior linguistic talent. His Black poems are characterized by verbal pyrotechnics, precision in the use of symbolism, brilliantly conceived metaphors, and immense imagination. In addition to his wholesome and sincere relationships with persons of African descent in and around his native Guayana, he read about Africa and African themes. He read José Más's In the Land of the Bubis, René Maran's descriptions of the Congo, and Frobenius's The Black Decameron.

Miguel Enguídanos assures us that Palés did not cultivate Black poetry merely to set a mode or to be fashionable.[7] "It is true," says Enguídanos,

that he read certain books on Africa and Africans and was familiar with the poems of Vachel Lindsay, but his Songs of the Black (Tuntún de pasa y grifería) has an air of revolution, of discovery, of naked truth that emanates from deep within. His search for the soul of Blacks in the hidden corners of his own innner experiences enabled him to arrive at blackness in his verses. Palés has uncovered, as few have ever done, the Black man's personality. He describes it fully, in intuitive flashes, in many of his poems. Palés' Blacks are his own and those of his readers. He does not consider himself a defender of an oppressed race; instead, he merely underscores the superior qualities of the Black man. He emphasizes and transmits, above all, rhythmical sense, the sensitivity, the emotional character, the grace, the majesty, and the endurance of Black men and women.

The concern for the use of neo-African cadence and phonology can be noted in this stanza from Palés's "Black Town":

Someone lazily unravels
in the wind a monotonous song
reeking with u's that are drowned
in rafts of sleepy dipthongs
and elongated guttural sounds . . .

In the poem there are references to plant life, animal life, and the landscape of West Africa: cocoteros, aguazales, baobab, hipopótamo, elefante. The following lines give us an idea of the extraordinary rhythm in the Black poetry written by Palés:

> The soul of Africa goes vibrating
> in the fat *mariyandá* rhythm, gyrating.

"Black Dance," one of Palés's most famous poems, marked the definite triumph of rhythm and onomatopoeic expressions *(jitanjáfora)* in Afro-Spanish poetry.

> Calabó and bamboo,
> bamboo and calabó.
> The big rooster crows: "Cock-a-doodlc-doo."
> The big hen goes: "Cock-a-doo, doo."
> It's the hot sun that burns in Timbucktu.
> It's the Black dance of Fernando Poó.

It can be said that the Afro-Antillean verses of Palés exalt the concept of Blackness. In them, we note the great admiration and respect that the unforgettable poet from Guayana had for members of the Black race. He learned to appreciate the Black man's noble ways, and he was fascinated by the exquisite charm and beauty of Black and mulatto women. Evidence of the latter is found in the following verses, which are well-known throughout the Spanish-speaking world:

> Along the sun-lit Antillean street
> goes Tembandumba of Quimbamba.
> Leeward flower, Rose of Uganda,
> because of you, in frenzy without requite,
> the nanigo blood of the Antilles is afire.
> Haiti offers you its calabashes;
> on you, fiery suns Jamaica lavishes.
> Cuba tells you, "Do, Sugar-plum!"
> And Puerto Rico exclaims, "My Sweet Honey-comb!"

The Black man's majesty is described clearly in the following verses by Palés:

> Brave Blacks of the palm groves,
> Come, Babissa awaits you.
> The Great King of the Alligator and the Coconut,
> Before the burning fire,
> Tum-cutum, tum-cutum,
> Before the burning fire.

And in the following verses, Palés includes Black mythological elements:

> Father Ogún, mighty god of war,
> who wears well-polished boots,
> and whose footsteps cause the Earth to roar . . .
> Father Ogún. Oh! Father Ogún.

In order to exalt Black majesty, the poet from Guayana fused together the most heterogeneous elements. Perhaps these elements were lacking anthropological or historical precision, but they made poetic sense. Unlike many writers of Black-inspired poetry, Palés did not willfully ridicule Blacks. Enguídanos says, "When the Black man loses the majesty of being Black he imitates the white man. Only then, when he wants to stop being what he is, when he forgets the grace and beauty of being Black, does Palés make fun of the Black man." Examples of such mockery are Palés's "Green Lizard" and "The Elegy of the Duke of Marmelade," in which the poet satirizes Haitian royalty. Here is a fragment of the former poem:

> Just watch him dance. He struts his gait
> in a rigadoon or minuet.
> None of those near Christophe the Great
> Wears half so well the robes of state,
> Moves with more genteel etiquette.
> His social formula: "S'il vous plait."
> His word of elegance: "Volupté."
>
> Ah, but before His Highness, never,
> Never say lizard, or you'll see
> That in one instant gone forever
> Is every trace of aristocracy.

In "Mixture" ("Ten con ten"), Palés spoke of the harmonious racial integration — Spanish, Indian, and African — that has taken place in Puerto Rico, a factor that influences the character and personality of the inhabitants of the beautiful Caribbean island.

Since the majority of the critics of poesía negra have tended to accentuate only a limited portion of this poetry, many people do not know that there are two other types of Afro-Spanish poetry which are no less important than the humorous poems and the folk poems. They are the social and the lyrical poems. It is important to note that the jitanjáfora (onomatopoeia), one of the most important ingredients of Afro-Spanish poetry, may be found in all four types of poemas negros. This could explain, in part, the neglect of social or lyrical poetry. Then too, some of the social poems are hard-biting and cynical in tone. Emilio Ballagas's poem "Attitude," a poem of bitter social protest, is a work which the author later regretted having written. Of course, there was lit..e or no opposition to poesía negra until it was used as an instrument of protest. It was then that a few influential literary critics began to feel that it exaggerated the importance of Blacks in Latin American life.

Afro-Antillean poetry, as a New World creation, is just as important as any other literary movement that originated in the New World, including the *Modernista* movement. If the poesía negra is denied serious critical attention and acclaim it is necessary to deny these to all the other types of indigenous Spanish American poetry. In the Spanish-speaking countries of Latin America, Black poetry of a social nature was born of the necessity to react to the hypocrisy of some poets who, without having felt the Black man's age-old sufferings and sorrows, attempted to pose as the torchbearers of the oppressed race. However, poesía negra had to engage in social criticism if it was to reflect faithfully every aspect of Black life. The history of the Black man in America, notwithstanding a few truly heroic and glorious moments, has been one of heartfelt sorrow and bitter suffering. The transplanted sons and daughters of Africa sought in song and religion an antidote for their deep-rooted pain and sorrow, their many unshed tears, and their infinite sadness. In the vast plantations of the Southern United States and in the cane fields of the Caribbean, the song was often mournful and the religious feeling very deep. From Black songs and emotions stemmed the *versos negros.* The socialistic Afro-Spanish poems are good when written by a poet who is sincere, but they are bad when inspired by the thorn of hypocrisy.

As for terminology, it would be well to bear in mind that there is no such thing as social poetry; there is only poetry. . . . The term "social" or "socialistic" poetry is used here solely to label a specific type of Black poetry. Socialistic Afro-Spanish poetry has three main themes: poverty, social injustice, and degradation. Although poverty is not unknown to any of the races of mankind, New World Blacks seem to have more than their share of it. It reaches such dimensions that Black Spanish-Americans consider it a curse of destiny. The social theme has given rise to different protest movements in the United States, in the Caribbean, and in West Africa. Social poetry written by neo-African poets inspired the poets of Negritude to write poems in support of African independence. Black African writers from Portugal's West African colonies mention the names of Hughes, Guillén, Palés, Damas, and Césaire in poems which support their struggle for independence.

West Indies Ltd. (Havana, 1934), one of Guillén's most important works, includes a number of protest poems, as does an earlier work by Guillén entitled *Motivos de son* (Havana, 1930). The following poem is from the latter book, which in English would be called *Son Themes:*

CANE

Black man
In the cane fields.

White man
Above the cane fields.

Earth
Beneath the cane fields

Blood
That flows from us.

"Balada de los dos abuelos" ("Ballad of the Two Grandfathers"), "Dos niños" ("Two Boys"), "Balada del güije" ("Ballad of the Water-Spirits"), and "Sabás" are other of Guillén's poems of social protest.

The poem "Actitud" ("Attitude") by Ballagas has already been mentioned as a militant poem. Two other noteworthy militant poems by Cuban poets of the poesía negra movement are "Evohé," by Marcelino Arozarena, and "Hermano negro," by Regino Pedroso. Both poems were inspired by the Scottsboro Case. The Colombian Manuel Rodríguez Cardenas has written several Black poems that are highly militant in tone. Other poems of the poesía negra movement that deal with the social theme are "Ballad of the Black Girl," by the Argentinean Luis Cané; "Black Man of America," by the Dominican Manuel del Cabral; "Old Black Man of the Port," by another Dominican, Francisco Rodríguez Charro; "Paint Me, Little Black Angels," by the Venezuelan Andrés Eloy Blanco; "It's a Small Thing To Be Black," by José Muñoz Costa, a Mexican; and "A Black Puerto Rican in the South," which Cesáreo Rosa-Nieves includes in his book of Black poems entitled *Black Tuning-Fork.*

In the Afro-Spanish poems of social protest, it is not uncommon for the poet to satirize his Black characters slightly or to criticize them strongly, for the sake of goading them to take positive steps for bettering their social conditions. Guillén does this with "Sabás," while in "Hermano negro" Pedroso tells his Black brother to silence his bongo a bit and begin the struggle against injustice. Arozarena, in "Evohé," tells his Black brothers and sisters to think a little about Scottsboro and not about Ogún.

Readers who take the time to examine Afro-Antillean poetry of Spanish expression rather closely will find that its range of themes is very rich and varied. The poesía negra includes much more than African or pseudo-African rhythms and expressions, much more than grotesque gestures and simian capers for provoking white laughter, and much more than jiving, high-stepping Black carousers. It contains much more than sinewy, vivacious, voluptuous, and carefree Black and mulatto women who light the lamps of love. Afro-Spanish poetry includes much more than references to superstitions and religious practices from the Dark Continent, the cries of street-vendors, legends, Black lullabies, or chants for killing a snake. María Belén Chacón, Mari Sabel, the Duke of Marmelade, the Count of Lemonade, Poppa Montero, and Yelidá are interesting figures, but they do not constitute the poesía negra in its entirety.

In the vast panorama of the poesía negra, among jokes and caricatures, there is a profound tragedy that is centuries old. Yet, there is to be found in this poetry a beauty that seems unsurpassable. The poesía negra is capable of attaining the most subtle expressions of esthetic refinement. Its beautiful lyrical tone manifests itself in rich, authentic metaphors. From the pen of Guillén is this metaphor: "Dark alligator waters." In the Afro-Cuban poet's "Ballad of the Water-Spirit" are these lines:

> Under the stars that holler,
> Under a moon afire,
> Among the stones barks a river,
> And strangles passersby.

When mockery and satire are cast aside, and when the poet eschews local color as his sole source of inspiration, the poesía negra reaches unsuspected lyrical heights. It continues, however, to be Black poetry, because it is still moved and inspired by that which is African.

Black poetry has been elevated to lofty peaks of lyricism by Spanish-speaking writers of different ethnic backgrounds. Federico García Lorca, who during a visit to Cuba was highly impressed by the *poemas negros,* wrote several Black poems. "The King of Harlem" is an interesting poem from Lorca's *Poet in New York.* Manuel Machado, Rafael Alberti, and Alfonso Camín are also among the Spanish poets who joined the poesía negra movement.

The following stanza is from one of Camín's poems:

> An H-shaped bridge of palms
> spans the night of the lagoon,
> your jet beauty without qualms
> is dazzling beneath the moon.

Modern Afro-Spanish poetry is definitely pure, beautiful, and interesting. It is faithful to its poetic mission, which is singing neo-African glories and announcing a new dawn. In it, the concept of blackness achieves greatness and splendor.

NOTES

1. Fernando Oritz, *Estudios africanos,* Vol. I (Havana, 1937), pp. 156-159.
2. Ciudad Trujillo, 1942.
3. Fernando Ortiz, *Los bailes y el teatro de los negros en el folklore de Cuba* (Havana, 1951).
4. *baquiné:* a wake for a small Black child.
5. Cesáreo Rosa-Nieves, "Luis Palés Matos: poeta del hastío, el pesimismo y la ironía," *Semana,* IX, no. 270 (Feb., 1957).
6. Juan Marinello, *Poética, ensayos de entusiasmo* (Madrid), p. 99.
7. *La poesía de Luis Palés Matos* (Río Piedras: Ediciones de la Universidad de Puerto Rico, 1961), pp. 59-60.

CONSTANCE SPARROW
de GARCÍA BARRIO

The Image of the Black Man in the Poetry of Nicolás Guillén

Prior to the beginning of the twentieth century, the image of blacks in Spanish-American literature had been limited to a few prototypes. This repertoire included the black as a physical dynamo, the meek and loyal slave, the sexually stirring mulatto woman, and the brave Afro-Spanish-American soldier fighting in the service of colonial authorities. Blacks themselves, during the colonial period, were rarely in a position to contribute to the making of their own literary image. They found themselves hindered by the lack of means to become literate since their learning to read and write was discouraged. If they managed to gain these skills, societal and governmental restrictions compelled them to write on themes alien to their own situation. Noting the predicament of blacks in colonial Cuba, G. Brown Castillo indicates that silence was the safest policy, and that intrepid writers "immediately exposed themselves to persecutions and torture by the existing regime."[1]

About 1900, a Negro vogue began in Europe. It seemed to provide an external stimulus for the study of blacks in Latin America, and their incorporation in literary works. In the late 1920s and early 1930s, Cuban writers, especially poets, avidly sketched black protagonists, but hardly ventured beyond the caricatures and customs presented in colonial literature. Moreover, for most of these writers, the inclusion of black characters represented no more than a parenthesis in their careers.

The Cuban mulatto poet Nicolás Guillén (1902–) proves an exception. He is the only major practitioner of Negroid poetry in whom the figure of the black man outlives the vogue of the first third of this century. Furthermore, during his career the poet has created black figures new to Spanish-American literature. These creations dynamically express the intense social concern and heightened political consciousness of the author. This essay will examine the genesis of these new black figures, and the ideas to which they give substance.

In 1930 Nicolás Guillén published his first collection of Negroid poems, *Motivos de son*. In it, he offers a potpourri of dark island types. While highly chromatic, this presentation of the lower strata of Cuban blacks is quite traditional in its predominant eight-syllable line, and in its reproduction of the peculiarities of the Spanish spoken by these islanders as well:

¿Por qué te pone tan bravo,	Why do you get so mad,
cuando te dicen negro bembón,	when they call you "Big-Lips,"
si tiene la boca santa,	because your mouth is sweet
negro bembón?	Big-Lips?
Bembón así como ere	Big Lips just as you are
tiene de to	you have everything
Caridad te mantiene,	Caridad supports you
te lo da to.[5]	you have everything.

As significant as the dropping of the final *s* of *pones, tienes,* and *eres,* and the reduction of *todo* to *to* is the theme of identity. The *bembón,* or big-lipped Black, objects to the epithet in spite of its accuracy. The poet contends that the bembón's mouth is large but sweet, and he has no grounds for complaint since he is being supported by his sweetheart Caridad. In another poem, Guillén reproves a mulatto woman who has laughed at his broad nose and called it a *nudo de corbata,* knot of a necktie. He replies that he would prefer his black gal to her any time.

In his next collection, *Sóngoro Cosongo* (1931), Guillén seems to divide his efforts between traditional black characters, and the shaping of new types. "Rumba" and "Secuestro de la mujer de Antonio" both capture the sexual implications of the rumba danced by a mulata. The knife-wielding *chévere,* prefigured in the *negro curro* of colonial literature,[2] is the subject of "Velorio de papá montero." The poem "Chévere" provides a briefer statement on the same type. Although *Sóngoro Cosongo* and *Motivos de son* share traditional elements, the former lacks the apparent lightheartedness of the latter. This new sobriety is conveyed in the elimination of dialect, in an ironic address to the question of racial identity, and in a concern over the exploitation of Cuba by the United States. One of the most striking poems in *Sóngoro Cosongo* is "Caña." Its terse lines denounce American economic control, its effect on the land where sugar cane is grown, and the anonymous black who cultivates it.

Guillén examines the United States from another vantage point in "Small Ode to a Cuban Boxer." He warns the boxer, who is about to travel to New York, that, "The North is wild and crude." The boxer's English is precarious, and his Spanish not much less so, but the poet tellingly suggests that the fighter's fists are what he will need to "speak black Truth."

Guillén presages the coming of a new breed of physically and morally superior men who will rise to claim what is rightfully due them. He portrays these men in "Arrival":

> Ah, comrades, here we are!
> Beneath the sun
> our sweaty skin will reflect the moist faces of the vanquished,
> and during the night, while stars burn on the tip of our flames,
> our laughter will wake on rivers and birds.[3]

Guillén presents the black woman as belonging to a group from which little has been heard, but from which everything positive may now be expected:

> The black woman, new woman
> comes forth in her light robe of snake skin.
> she brings the unspoken word
> the strong buttocks,
> the voice, the tooth, the morning, and the leap.

Three years later, in *West Indies Ltd.* (1934), the poet's attitude has become much more aggressive. Allusions to the clenched fist, later to be the symbol of the Black Power Movement, fill this collection. He asks why the fists of the dock workers haven't been raised in a single decisive gesture:

> Oh strong fist, elemental and hard!
> Who restrains your open gesture?

In "Ballad of Simón Caraballo," a black beggar sings his sorrows, but the lines that spotlight his hands reveal anger and potential violence:

> I
> black Simon Caraballo,
> sleep on a door step now;
> a brick is my pillow
> my bed is on the ground.
> . . . . . .
> . . . . . .
> I don't know what to do with my arms
> but I'll find something to do
> I,

> black Simon Caraballo,
> have my fists closed,
> have my fists closed,
> and I need to eat!

In describing another black, Sabás, who begs from door to door, the poet poses the question three times: "Why, Sabás, the open hand?" He urges Sabás to demand what he needs, and discard his open-handed attitude:

> Get your bread, but don't beg for it;
> Get your light, get your rightful hope
> like a horse by the reins.
> Stand right in the middle of the door,
> but not with an open hand
> nor with your prudence of a fool:

Guillén chose to invest another poor black character with his most urgent message in 1937, when *Songs for Soldiers and Tunes for Tourists* was published. This figure is distinctive in his immunity to the venality associated with the tourist trade. A musician, he warns the tourists that his song, unlike that of many of his countrymen, will not soothe them like the rum they drink because José Ramón Cantaliso — perhaps the artist's self-portrait — is a singer-of-truths:

> In bars, parties, gatherings,
> to the tourists on all fours
> and to the natives as well,
> to all, the necessary tune
> José Ramón Cantaliso
> sings clearly, very clearly,
> so that they can understand him well.

One of Cantaliso's songs describes a "Solar," or seedy tenement house,[4] and its occupants, mentioning specifically those who are black:

> And this one is Luis, the candy vendor;
> And this one is Carlos, the islander;
> and that black
> is named Pedro Martínez,
> and that other one,
> Noberto Soto
> and that black woman over there,
> Petra Sarda
> They all live in one room,
> probably
> because it's cheaper that way.
> What people
> What mindful people!

The model of the singer-of-truth, whose voice has grown more strident, reappears in "Son venezolano," from *El son entero* (1947). This time he bears the name Juan Bimba, and makes a frontal attack on foreign exploitation of Cuban and Venezuelan products:

> I sing in Cuba and Venezuela,
> a song that comes out of me.
> What bitter oil,
> caramba,
> oh, how bitter this oil,
> caramba,
> that tastes like Cuban sugar!

In *El son entero*, Guillén pours the seething anger of the beggars into a new vessel, that of the rebellious slave. The enslaved black, who has been recovering from a beating, rises to slay his master in "Sweat and Whip":

> Then the silent sky,
> and under the sky, the slave
> stained in the blood of the master.

Violent self-assertion would inform some of Guillén's later black figures too. This position is summarized in "Sports," a poem from *La paloma de vuelo popular* (1958). The poem contains a catalogue of black prize fighters from both Americas,

> But above all, I think
> of the Patent-Leather Kid, the great king without a crown
> and of Chocolate, the great crowned king,
> and of Black Bill, with his rubber nerves.

Guillén implies that their victories as individuals are enhanced by the pride they inspire in other blacks. Repeated mention of the Cuban chess grandmaster José Raul Capablanca seems to countervail the importance given to physical stamina. Intellectual vigor is also necessary.

During this period, racism in the United States, with its concomitants of segregation in schools and lynching, claimed Guillén's attention. In "Little Rock" and "Elegy to Emmett Till," the poet gives voice to his indignation. "Elegy to Emmett Till" was written for a fourteen-year-old black who was lynched in Greenwood, Mississippi, in 1955. It minutely describes a "danse macabre" over the mutilated body of the boy:

with white men dancing
in a cannibal light,
and nocturnal bonfires
with a black man always burning:
the obedient Black,
his torn bowels wrapped in smoke,
his guts choked with fumes,
his abused sex . . .
there in the alcoholic South,
there in the South of insult and lash.[5]

Guillén also wrote an elegy for the Haitian poet Jacques Roumain, whose poetry is as militant as his own. Another elegy was written for Jesús Menéndez, an organizer of Cuban sugar workers, who was murdered in 1948. The poem constitutes a counterpoint of murder and the American business interests which triggered it:

At last the ruptured artery,
blood reported one morning
on the New York
Stock Exchange.

In 1959, the revolution of Fidel Castro triumphed. One of its goals, the eradication of racial discrimination,[6] was accomplished through the immediate integration of schools and all public facilities. Guillén jubilantly reflects on the changes wrought by the revolution in *Tengo*, written in 1964:

I have, let's see
that being a black man
no one can stop me
at the door of a bar or of a dance hall
Nor in the vestibule of a hotel
scream at me that there's no vacancy.

With the achievement of institutionalized equality in Cuba,[7] Guillén seems to focus on the situation of blacks in the United States. This explains the lapidary note on the cage of one of the animals in *El gran zoo* (1967). The beast in question is the Ku Klux Klan:

This quadruped comes
from Joplin, Missouri.
Carnivorous.
It howls long into the night
without its habitual diet of roasted black.
In the end it will die.
Feeding it is the (insoluble) problem.[8]

Still directing his attention towards the United States, Guillén included a poem in praise of the will and militancy of Angela Davis. Although it appears in *La rueda dentada* (1972), it depicts the heroine as being made of the same elemental stuff that gave strength to the "New Woman" of 1931:

> How your executioners mislead themselves!
> You are made of rough and glowing stuff,
> a rustproof impulse,
> capable of lasting through suns and rains,
> through winds and moons
> in the unsheltered air.
> You belong to
> that class of dreams in which time
> has always forged its statues
> and written its songs.[9]

A poem dedicated to Martin Luther King also appears in this volume. It comes as a reply to the Russian poet Evtuchenko, who described King as a black man with ". . . a most pure soul like white snow." Guillén, in his violent rejection of this image, ends his poem by saying that King's soul was "black like coal." Guillén was understandably provoked by the use of the words "white snow" to describe a black man who had lived many of the ideals that Guillén saw as essential. For more than forty years, Nicolás Guillén has forcefully treated blacks in his poetry. During that time, one can observe a transition from the presentation of the usual black figures, speaking in a typically distorted manner, poured into the traditional octosyllabic lines, to the naissance of startling new blacks, whose profiles are often etched in free verse.

Guillén seems to begin by making plastic his vision of ideal men and women in "Arrival" and "New Woman." Once the ideal has been described, the poet proceeds to grapple with raw reality. Thus emerge the black beggars. Guillén would make of his poems a *maraca* or *güire*, a percussion instrument whose beat would awaken the beggars to a sense of self-worth and the need to fight. He tells them to demand a share of society's goods rather than beg for them. The tone of this poetry grows increasingly tense and combative, and may be summed up in the clenched fist, an image which appears repeatedly.

A third new black figure is the singer-of-truth, José Ramón Cantaliso. Poverty has made him hypersensitive to the economic ills that the tourist trade has brought to Cuba. His song stresses the suffering of poor Cubans, and while the tune does not please the tourist's ear, it cannot be changed by their dollars. Later, the song of Juan Bimba, a character in every way similar to José Ramón Cantaliso, denounces parasitic foreign business interests in the Caribbean.

In much of Guillén's later poetry, there seems to be a conformity between the black figures he has drawn earlier and the concrete men and
women whom he makes the subject of his poems. The premium which
Guillén places on physical strength and an indomitable spirit is incarnated
in Kid Charol, Kid Chocolate, Johnson, and Black Bill, all of whom are
boxers. These traits are also seen in Jesús Menéndez, who sought power for
the Cuban sugar workers through organization. His mission was parallel
to that of Cantaliso, who aimed to jar tourists and islanders out of the old
pattern with his song. Angela Davis and Martin Luther King also provide
living examples of the militancy and purpose that Guillen has placed in
some of his fictional figures.

In assessing Guillén's contribution to Spanish American literature,
Cuba's long colonial status must be kept in mind. In 1898, the island was
freed from Spanish domination only to immediately become a functional
protectorate of the United States. Frantz Fanon, in discussing the shift
from colonial mentality to national consciousness, states that the change
is usually accompanied by a break with past artistic expression. When
commenting on creative trajectories similar to that of Guillén, he states:

. . . the progress of national consciousness among the people modifies
and gives precision to the literary utterances of the native intellectual.
The continued cohesion of the people constitutes for the intellectual an
invitation to go further than his cry of protest. The lament first makes the
indictment; then it makes an appeal. In the period that follows, the words
of command are heard. The crystallisation of the national consciousness
will both disrupt literary styles and themes, and also create a completely
new public.[10]

Although Guillén has forged new types, he has written a variety of
other poems of ethnic content as well. On occasion, he has delved into
Afro-Spanish folklore and religion. He also wrote a lullaby for a black
baby, conspicuous because of its late date of publication, 1958. The question of racial identity is handled in various guises throughout his career.
Guillén never loses historical perspective, as "Noche de negros junto a la
catedral" (1966) reveals. His creation of new figures and the cultivation
of other Afro-Spanish themes measure the depth of his commitment.

NOTES

1. *Cuba colonial* (Havana: Jesús Montero, 1952), p. 56.
2. Cirilo Villaverde, *Cecilia Valdés* (Mexico: Editorial Porrúa, S.A., 1972), pp. 245–247.
3. Translated by Robert Marquez and David Arthur McMurray, *Manmaking Words* (Amherst: University of Massachusetts Press, 1972), pp. 143–145.
4. David W. Ames, "Negro Family Types in a Cuban Solar," *Phylon* 11 (1950), p. 160. This study of a "solar" in Havana shows that in the 90 rooms of the building, 462 people lived. 141 were white and 321 were black.
5. Translated by Robert Marquez and David Arthur McMurray.
6. William J. Parente, "The Red & the Black," *Problems of Communism*, July-Aug., 1970, p. 47.
7. Elizabeth Sutherland, "Colony within the Colony," *The Youngest Revolution: A Personal Report on Cuba* (New York: Dial Press, Inc., 1969), p. 146. All public facilities and educational institutions have been integrated, but prejudice has survived in subtle ways, particularly among members of the older generations.
8. N. Guillén, "KKK", *El Gran Zoo* (Buenos Aires: Talleres Gráficos Callao, 1967), p. 39.
9. N. Guillén, "Angela Davis," *La Rueda Dentada* (Havana: Instituto Cubano del Libro, 1972), pp. 32–33. Translated by R. Marquez and D. A. McMurray, *Man-making Words*, pp. 187–189.
10. Frantz Fanon, *The Wretched of the Earth* (New York: Grove Press, Inc., 1971), p. 193.

MIRIAM DeCOSTA

Social Lyricism and the
Caribbean Poet/Rebel

Before 1928 there were two distinct currents of Afro-Caribbean poetry —
the anonymous folk poetry of the people (slaves, field hands, and street
vendors) and the learned poetry of those who wrote in a consciously
literary style. The first neo-African poetry is to be found in the spontaneous and improvised songs — songs of praise, war chants, love songs, *letrillas*,
canciones and *coplas* — the poetry of unknown rustic bards who perpetuated the oral tradition which had been their African heritage. Many of the
short, four-lined coplas express pride in blackness, self-esteem and respect,
love of the Black woman, humor at the antics of white folk, who must be
placated and tolerated. One example is this Cuban copla about a tough
"macho" named Candela, who is ready and eager to defend himself with
his knife and razor:

> At this point Candela arrived,
> a breaking, splitting Black man,
> who whips out his knife
> and cuts with his switch blade.[1]

The theme of protest runs as a leitmotif through much of the Black
folk poetry of the Caribbean and South America; in Cuba, Ecuador or
Venezuela the dialect, the verse forms, the secondary themes — oppression,
cruelty, injustice, exploitation — attest to the universality of neo-African
folk poetry. For example, two poems from Uruguay — a freedom song and

"Social Lyricism and the Caribbean Poet/Rebel." From the *College Language Association Journal*, 15 (June, 1972), pp. 441–451. Reprinted by
permission of the *CLA Journal.*

a war chant – have their counterparts in the *cancioneros* of Cuba and Ecuador. In the freedom song, the poet proclaims that he was born free, having no other master than God, until the arrogant white man enslaved him like a beast.

> I want to be free
> for I was born free
> and I knew
> no other master than God.
> The arrogant white man
> with his inhuman arm
> punishes his brother
> like a fierce beast.[2]

The same fierce sense of independence, pride and militancy is evident in a Uruguayan marching song:

> We are fine Black men
> We are fighting men
> And as military men
> We want to fight
> For we leave to do combat
> And marching in force
> We die fighting
> for Liberty.[3]

None of the themes of protest – desire for freedom, complaint of suffering, rebellion against the inhumanity of the oppressor – which abound in folk poetry, are evident in the learned poetry of Blacks. Eighteenth-century writers like Juana Pastor, "a brown poetess and distinguished teacher," wrote sonnets and *décimas*, while her fellow Cuban, Manuel del Socorro Rodríguez, also composed innocuous verse.[4] The two most celebrated poets of the nineteenth century, Gabriel de la Concepción Valdés (Plácido) and Juan Francisco Manzano, illustrate the defects of the period – a period of imitation – for they patterned their writing after European romantics, omitting any reference in their poetry to personal experiences, attitudes and feelings. Plácido wrote sentimental, mediocre verse in which he assumed a literary pose – that of the poet / protestor – but his is a general protest against tyranny (unnamed), injustice (undefined) and oppression (unspecified), rather than a diatribe against slavery, the despotism of the Spanish colonialists, and the miseries of Black Cuban life. This type of general protest is evident in the poem "El juramento."

> To be the eternal enemy of tyranny,
> To stain, if possible, my clothes
> With blood drawn by my hand.

To spill it with repeated blows;
And to die at the hands of the executioner,
If it is necessary, to break the yoke.

Although Manzano was born a slave, as was Juan Latino (the Spanish poet, university professor and humanist of the seventeenth century), and was freed following the publication of his *Cantos a Lesbia*, neither slavery nor personal suffering is treated thematically in his verse.

In addition to Manzano and Plácido, there was a pleiade of lesser Afro-Cuban poets in the nineteenth century, and one scholar estimates that between 1815 and 1927 Black Cubans published some 402 books, pamphlets and newspapers.[5] However, none of these recorded the momentous impact of Blacks on Caribbean history — the slave insurrections of the eighteenth century; the first rebellions against the Spanish, the 1868 War of Yara and the heroism of the Black rebels, Maceo, Moncada, Crombet and Banderas; and the insurrection of 1895 by the "Mambises." Instead, the first Afro-Caribbean poets, like their counterpart, Phyllis Wheatley, in the United States, wrote romantic sonnets and classical odes; they did not protest or write about what they knew best — their suffering. The miracle is that they wrote at all. Enslaved, jailed, oppressed, refused schools, denied an education, Black men had to steal knowledge by candle-light from forbidden books.

In 1928, the publication of "La rumba" by José Tallet and "Bailadora de rumba" by Ramón Guirao introduced *negrismo* to Caribbean literature. The next decade saw a plethora of *negristas* writing about Black dancers, songs, rites, rituals and customs with resonances of sentimental romanticism, decadent naturalism, and a touch of *costumbrismo* at its worst. Poets reproduced exotic scenes, colors, sounds and rhythms, selecting Spanish words for sounds rather than meaning and inventing nonsense words *(jitanjáfora)* for their onomatopoeic value. Writers familiar with the works of Fernando Ortiz, the social anthropologist, and Lydia Cabrera, a folklorist, incorporated African folklore and mythology — the orishas, or deities, of *Santería* and *Nañiguismo* — into their poetry. This early period can be characterized as one in which whites mimicked Blacks without even an elementary understanding of the nature of the Black experience. It was poetry about people viewed from without, superficially, from the perspective of the Sartrian "Other." The *negrista* poets were essentially European in their point of view, their values and their esthetic, while they considered everything African to be "savage" and "primitive."

It is the Afro-Cuban poets — Guillén, Arozarena and Pedroso — who infuse meaning, content and significance into this poetry as they use the Spanish language to convey, lyrically, the neo-African experience.

Regino Pedroso, a Cuban of African and Chinese descent, eschewed the esthetic of "art for art's sake," committing himself, instead, to the political and social liberation — through poetry — of his people. Guillén, in his introduction to Pedroso's *Poemas: antología,* esteems the poet's strong, grandiose, authentically Cuban social poetry, poetry forged of ironlike blows with rhythmic form and free verse. *Nosotros* incorporates many of the themes of social protest — poverty, personal suffering, social problems, hunger — treated by Caribbean poets of the Thirties. However, Pedroso's protest is more social than racial, for he writes about the masses, the lumpenproletariat (Blacks, Chinese, Indians), all the workers of the factories, cane fields and sugar plants where he grew to manhood. His is the authentic voice of the rebel, and not the weak lament of the literary poseur.

Like so many poets of the Thirties, his sense of outrage (for he says his soul was forged in hatred of social injustices) led him to Marxism, and he declares himself to be a Marxist revolutionary, thus anti-capitalist, anti-imperialist, and profoundly anti-American. The anti-Yankee theme (with its modern equivalent: "Cuba, sí; Yanki, no") predominates in poetry of this period, for Cubans found that they had gained independence from Spain in 1898 only to fall victim to another colonial power, the United States. Pedroso condemns the Slaves of Progress on the barbarian continent, where men head for Wall Street with a load of dollars on their backs. In "Ours is the Land," he exhorts his Cuban brothers: "Leave them with their dollars, with their tickets and their Wall Street. Leave them with their gods and their luxury, for their luxury is borrowed and they are dressed with our misery."

Pedroso also attacks military exploitation (called *miguelismo* in South America after the Black hero "El Rey Miguel," who fought for the liberation of Venezuela), because men fight to liberate their country, only to be treated as slaves when they return home. Pedroso denounces miguelismo, because the poor and the Black are used, exploited and killed in the wars of liberation without ever reaping the fruits of their victory. In his poem "There Will be War Again" he protests:

> We will die abroad
> And we will return slaves;
> they will wave the same flags of freedom
> and we will still be slaves.
> We will be conquering heroes
> but we will be hungry.
> Until one day
> we will ask ourselves with brutal anger
> if we have fought for something.

In the poems of Pedroso, man is enslaved by the military-industrial complex, by the machinery of exploitative Yankee capitalist imperialism, or what an Ecuadorian poet calls simply "economic slavery." But Pedroso does not forget that this more modern, more subtle, but just as corrosive form of slavery, originated some four hundred years before, when the slave ships touched the banks of the Senegal and Gambia rivers. And so, he speaks of his ancestral Africa and China as two dismembered, conquered continents. He remembers the *tumbeiros* (the "coffins" or slave ships) in his "Ballad in Ship-Wrecked Lands":

> A ship! A ship from the North!
> ships along the black coasts!

He writes in an almost surrealistic style, like Rimbaud in his "Bateau d'Ivre," of the imperialists, memories of the whip, and a slave ship from Wall Street.

Pedroso protests Black oppression and racial exploitation in his celebrated poem "Black Brother." This poem was inspired by the travesty of American justice that was Scottsboro; for many Caribbean writers, like Guillén and Arozarena, were shocked and outraged by what was happening to their Black brothers in the land of Jim Crow. They wrote not only of Scottsboro, but also of the lynchings, the assassinations of Black leaders, the murder of Emmett Till and others. Underlying much of this type of protest poetry is another theme — the appeal for Black brotherhood, solidarity, a united front in the face of oppression. Sometimes, as in the case of Pedroso, the ideological appeal was for a Third-World union — a union based not necessarily on race but on the oppression experienced by all the downtrodden. In the first stanza of "Hermano negro," Pedroso speaks of a oneness, saying: "You are in me; I am in you," the implication being that it is a oneness of the flesh, for he speaks of "our blood." It is also a oneness of the spirit, based on shared sorrows, our "angustia," the experience of mutual suffering in a hostile world. What is the essence of this Black spirit? Pedroso implies that it lies in two contradictory poles, expressed in song and lament, the joy / sorrow dichotomy of the blues — the "minute to smile and hour to weep in."

The entire history of the Black man is recounted in three stanzas: first, there was the peace that was Africa, where man was free, like the animals and the trees, the rivers and the suns. Then there was the slavery of the New World, where the whip burned the flesh. Now there is that other slavery, that slavery of the spirit — a worldwide system, European, American and Caribbean-based, where rich men fabricate Blacks without guts, strawmen, invisible men. Like puppets who dance to someone else's tune, Blacks laugh, dance, sing, scratch their heads and shuffle. The real question is posed in the stanza which begins: "Tu amaste?" The poet asks "Are you real, Black brother? Didn't you love at least once? Didn't you shout one time? Didn't you live just once?" In other words, "Aren't you more than just straw?" We must listen, watch and learn in the example of Scottsboro. Blacks in Haiti, in Jamaica, in New York and Havana must protest; the Black man must still his maracas and scream his rebel anger throughout the world.

The best expression of Pedroso's view of the Black experience, of his political ideology and his poetic creed is to be found in his "Auto-bio-prólogo" to *Nosotros:*

Born in a country that is politically and economically enslaved by Yankee imperialism, classified by traditional concepts of bourgeois religion, philosophy and science, as a member of an inferior Ethiopian-Asiatic race, belonging to the proletariat, the most oppressed and exploited of classes, what can be my ideology, with such a geographic, historic, ethnic and socio-economic destiny? That that comes from Marx, finds its synthesis in Lenin, and is moved in the world by International Justice. Objective and philosophy: to contribute to the affirmation of a social lyricism in the new lands of America.

Pedroso proposes a social lyricism, and he is, indeed, a social poet, a rebel poet!

Less of a rebel, perhaps, but just as much a poet is Marcelino Arozarena, who in the early Thirties received a copy of Pedroso's *Nosotros* and of Guillén's second work, *Sóngoro Cosongo*. These works had a profound impact on the young poet, as he states in the introduction to his own collection of verse, *Canción negra sin color:* "I intend to sing as a Black man, but with the voice that reaches all of us in the universal song." Indeed, the title of his work, "Black Song Without Color," indicates that Arozarena writes from the personal perspective of the Black, but he sings of that aspect of the Black experience which is universal, not hermetic.

So, Arozarena's song of rebellion is in a minor key, pianissimo, with muted tones and softer resonances. His song, however, is not the jubilant song and dance of the negrista poets. For in the poem from which the book takes its title, the poet writes: "We are flesh, song — the Ninth Symphony of Revolution." Arozarena points up the irony of the joy song; he speaks of "looping the loop of jubilation, while there in the hangars of the future is Hunger" with a capital "H." In his poem "Justicia" he uses the game of dominoes, metaphorically, and in a play on the words "dominó" (the game) and the preterite of *dominar* (to dominate) states: "I too serve to dominate (or to win at dominoes)." He speaks prophetically of a time to come — a time of revindication, when he won't be despised because he's poor (or has shot a double blank), a time when we will all be equal.

The most militant poem of Arozarena is "Evohé (a cry of the Roman Bacchants)," and, like Pedroso's "Hermano negro," this was inspired by the Scottsboro incident. Arozarena, like Pedroso and Guillén, warns Black people not to buy the white man's image of them, not to accept oppression, but to rise up, to rebel. His poem is an appeal to the dignity, to the worth, to the heroism of Black people. Arozarena says: "think a little about Scottsboro and not about Ogún" (the Yoruba *orisha* or deity of iron). In essence he says, "think of the hard reality of today and not the mythic past, the world of Afro-Cuban folklore." He exalts the Black man, his power, proclaiming: "Your voice is dynamite and not tourist laughter with a rumba beat; your dance enslaves you, for your steps are whiplashes." His "suelta el bongó" (throw away your bongo) is reminiscent of Pedroso's admonition to "quiet the maracas." Similar in theme to "Evohé" is "Carnaval de Santiago," where Arozarena precludes the passive, non-violent role in favor of a decidedly militant stance, declaring: "If the land that you feed, doesn't want to feed you, kick it. Throw off the flesh that's dying from so much waiting. Throw off the soul that's dying from so much dreaming. Throw off the voice that's dying from so much silence." Finally, he concludes: "The drum of the cool rumba is bathed in the sorrow of the people."

Nicolás Guillén is one of the most prolific and one of the finest poets of the Afro-Cuban movement. Now some seventy years old, Guillén continues to write, with such works as *Tengo* and *El Gran Zoo* being published in the late Sixties. He is president of the Cuban Writers' Union, and serves as his country's Minister of Culture. Imamu Baraka talks of conversations with the poet during his trip to Cuba, in a collection of essays called *Home*. A detailed study of Guillén's poetry, which spans four decades, reveals the evolution of a poet / rebel. His first two works follow the trend set by the negrista poets of the late Twenties: emphasis on plasticity (color and movement), rhythm through selection and repetition of sounds, musicality, Afro-Cuban dialect, themes from African folklore, etc. Some of his best-known poems are of this period, but even in this early stage of his development, the theme of social protest is a strong underlying current in his poetry. One poem, "Caña," from his first work, *Motivos de son* (1930), will illustrate:

> Black man
> stuck to the cane field
> Yankee
> over the cane field
> Earth
> under the cane field
> Blood flowing out of us

This is sharp, bleak, cutting poetry. The images strike out. There are few adjectives, little description — none of the sentimental, decadent, sugar coating of the negrista poets.

In his later works, these characteristics of Guillén's poetic style are accentuated, as the man becomes more rebellious, strident, forceful and impatient. His work includes all the themes of protest — those treated by his contemporaries, Arozarena and Pedroso, and others as well: slavery, refusal to join Third-World white revolutionaries, disillusionment with Cuban politics, anti-imperialism, identification with the poor and the hungry, proletarian revolution, protest against injustice (particularly in the U.S.), sympathy for American Blacks, and even criticism of marriage as a form of subjugation. As his political ideology took form, he moved toward socialism and communism, as did Pedroso. He purified his poetry even more, developing a tough, realistic style. There is none of the pseudo-African *paisaje* (the palm trees and crocodiles that had colored the super-ficial verse of poets like Palés Matos). He "reifies," using concrete substan-tives like earth, heat, bodies, blood. His poetry is spontaneous, like the lives of Black people, and his words are simple, like the language of the folk. He de-lyricizes his poetry, developing an almost prose style that hits, explodes, screams, like the poetry of Black American poets of the late Sixties and early Seventies. He eschews the personal, the subjective, the "I," in favor of the plural, the collective voice, the "we." In Guillén's poetry the form (style, language and structure) *in*-forms the content.

One example of Guillén's protest poetry, "West Indies Ltd.," sums up the attitude of these neo-African poets toward the Caribbean. The negristas viewed the Caribbean as white beaches under a tropic moon, where Negroes drink rum and dance the rumba in the nightclubs of Havana. Guillén, Arozarena and Pedroso pierce the surface to get to the guts of the tropics, to reach the harsh reality, where Black folk eke out a meager existence to the tune of the tourist dollars. *West Indies Ltd.* is a long poem which includes a portrait of the real Antilles, four *sones,* or song/dances, and a final epitaph.

In Part IV, the theme of hunger is directly associated with the Antilles; hunger stalks the city — a city of yellow faces and ghostly bodies. The *p* and *l* sounds of "pululando a pleno sol y a plena luna" onomato-poeically evoke the sounds of wolves, harbingers of death, howling in the night. In two short, succinct lines, the waterfront slums of Havana (or New York or Baltimore) materialize:

Night peopled by prostitutes
Bars peopled by sailors.

It is a world made hazy by the blur of alcohol and champagne, and the fuzziness of morphine, cocaine and heroin. And, as in Harlem or Watts or Hough, the police are ready to shoot the protester who complains that the bread is too hard or the soup too thin.

In Part VII, Guillén satirizes a bicultural, bilingual Cuba where the English of the Americans supersedes the Spanish of the Cubans, where the culture of the colonists dominates that of the colonized. Expressions like "ten cents," "all right," and "hello baby" convey the level of American culture.

Although the theme of protest has taken various forms — from the fighting militancy of the marching troops in the folk *copla,* to Arozarena's subjective and personal appeal for Black solidarity in the face of oppression, to Guillén's sharp, cutting, satire of the oppressors — the message is the same. The Afro-Caribbean poets warn, deride, criticize, ridicule, intimate, speak softly and strike hard, for their Ninth Symphony of Revolution is a call to arms.

NOTES

1. José Juan Arrom, "Presencia del negro en la poesía folklórica americana," *Certidumbre de América* (Havana, 1959), p. 111. Arrom notes that the copla is to be found in *Guarachas cubanas,* p. 58, and is also cited by Dolores María de Ximeno y Cruz in "Canciones populares en Cuba a mediados del siglo XIX," *Archivos del folklore cubano,* IV, no. 4 (Oct.-Dec. 1929), p. 357.
2. Horacio Jorge Becco, *Negros y morenos en el Cancionero Rioplatense,* 1953, pp. 39–40. Becco points out that the song was collected by Vicente Rossi, *Cosas de negros* (Río de la Plata, 1926), p. 115.
3. Becco notes that Ildefonso Pereda Valdés included it in his *Cancionero popular uruguayo* (Montevideo, 1947). Translated with the assistance of Stanley Cyrus, Howard University.
4. José Antonio Fernández de Castro, *Tema negro en las letras de Cuba (1608-1935)* (Havana, 1943), pp. 23-24.
5. *Ibid.,* p. 21.

LEMUEL JOHNSON

El Tema Negro:
The Nature of Primitivism in the
Poetry of Luis Palés Matos

> The hog in the mire grunts: oink, oink, oink.
> The frog in the pond goes: glug, glug, glug.
> . . . . .
> It is the iron sun that burns in Timbuctoo
> It is the black dance of Fernando Poo.
>
> — Luis Palés Matos, "Black Dance"

Palés Matos was not alone, of course. The period (the Twenties) was both repository and shaper of the romance evident in the *negrería fantasmal* of the Puerto Rican poet. It is this that, in part, makes Palés Matos's excursion into the *tema negro* the kind of reductive safari that it is — in effect, an artistic representation of one of the hyperbolic poses of the period. It may, perhaps, be New Criticism heresy to so categorically refer the poet and poetry to the coincidences of psychological and artistic energies which so significantly fixed the relevant decade in posed, exaggerated metaphors: Roaring Twenties and Jazz Age.

However, those years responded to the tema negro, at the level at which Palés Matos, Eugene O'Neill *(Emperor Jones)*, Blaise Cendrars *(Comment les Blancs sont d'anciens Noirs)*, Vachel Lindsay, et al., participated, with a plethora of assorted cries and echoistic alliterations which were, of course, plurisignificant. At one level, they constitute a poetics of primitivist romance; at another, they implicitly locate the quintessence of blackness in that romance. Romance is here not necessarily identified in the idyllic, though the Noble Savage aspect of the tema negro would provide that. The range of participants provided that primitivist romance with generic variety. We thus move through the Gothic Romance in the atavistic nakedness of O'Neill's *Emperor Jones* to the perhaps involuntary Romance as Fantasy-Farce offering of Palés Matos. At given stages one may even identify finer mutations — thus, the orchestration of pigs, frogs, roosters and hens — and the *raza negra* may be said to impinge on a variety of romance as Aesopian fantasy.

We may also rightly interpret these efforts as an extension of the period's fascination with vulgarity — either as subject or object, consciously or unconsciously animating the creative perception. In Scott Fitzgerald's archetypal (for this kind of romance) energization the world is fixed inside a syntax of hyperbolic vulgarity: that "ineffable gaudiness" of Gatsby-ism with its "vast, meretricious beauty." Corruption entertained in such hyperboles generates a seductive decadence which sets up a fine tension between the irony of moral perception and the negation of that irony in mythology. The discourse is thus exquisitely fixed on the threshold of a metaphysics of vulgarity, the appropriate or perhaps seemingly appropriate response to which is a near-religious sensuousness. (Norman Mailer's relationship to the body politic, fixing, as it does, the factor of vulgarity between two romantic archetypes – Saint George and the Godfather at the head of the Armies of the Night – is a contemporary illustration, an apocalyptic vision that weds a second-class Hieronymous Bosch/William Blake pose against (?) the contemporary reality.)

In *The Great Gatsby,* by the exercise of a barely successful fineness of irony, Fitzgerald again barely escapes from the mesmerizing "jazziness" of "the world as jazz." There is, perhaps, given the nature of the reaches of romance in the *tema negro,* a more elementary reason for the unconsummated hypnosis of the vulgar in *The Great Gatsby.* The ultimate moral referents (here defined as the unstated values that implicitly provide the basis for *The-Great-Gatsby-as-Satire*) are rooted in a dream of traditional Western/American Promise. The work concretizes these vague postulates in the perhaps mundane but still polyfacetedly discrete green light (precorruption or, if you will, pre-Fall).

There are no such steadying "green lights" which can animate and fix intelligent boundaries in the use of the *tema negro* by the Palés Matos school. In the final analysis, green, in the context of the *tema negro,* cannot imply an essentially sedate Eden but an unending, retrogressive explosion of nature on a rampage. The dynamics of stereotypical, percussive *jitanjáforas* insistently serve to locate and define the black theme in atavistic impulses from which no upward movement is possible. The use of the *tema negro* thus finds equilibrium in the simultaneous reduction of poetic creativity and insight to mechanical structures – indeed, the predictable clankiness of the poetic architecture *is* its measure of consummate skill. It is the acceptance of this premise that explains the extraordinary ability of Anderson Imbert to see in Palés Matos one of the most original poets of the modern era. But the devices used by Palés Matos, in the tema negro range, have been literarily ubiquitous (and predictable) in Spanish literature as early as Lope de Vega, Simón Aguado and, of course, Góngora – whenever they undertook poetic safaris in search of the quintessence of the *alma negra.* In this light, Angel Valbuena Prat's wide-eyed assertion, the "calabo and bamboo" of "Black Dance," the first three stanzas of "Nam-Nam," the cannibal dance or "Candombe," the "False Song of the Black Child's Wake," "Numen" and "Bombo" reveal a perfected style,

is meaningful only if it states a painfully obvious fact: the predictable and stereotypical derivativeness of Palés Matos's architecture. It is clear, however, that Valbuena Prat's "revelan todo un estilo" is intended to affirm the poet's creative originality.

One major consequence of all this is that in discussions of the peculiar ways in which the tema negro has manifested itself in Hispanic literature, the emphasis is on architecture. Insistently formalist criteria are offered − in both descriptive and prescriptive terms. Thus Arturo Torres-Rioseco compounds the issue by the somewhat exclamatory absolutes of his statement:

Negro poetry abandons the syllabic principle of Spanish versification; musical effects are based entirely on rhythm, and enhanced by alliteration, parallelism, onomatopoeia, internal rhyme, endless repetition of vowel sounds, and even musical instruments.

All this, of course, merely confirms *the* fact that "tal es la inclinación que los negros tienen a ser músicos" (Cervantes). Or, as Lorca would have it, "Ese negro que se saca la música hasta de los bolsillos!" Monochromatic musical architecture thus provides absolute prescription for "negro" poetry.

But the nature of the "music" in Torres-Rioseco's formulation is significant. A monochromatic, percussively unmodulatable music emerges; it is overtly simplistic in architecture, and, as a consequence (in the perception of the Palés Matos school), that architecture becomes one with what it houses. The range of emotions and insights which Palés Matos's *negrería* offers is perforce, one must assume, as monotonously conscribed as the vehicle of presentation. The poet as poet-creator "imitates" the nature of the *tema*. The tema as poetic persona also "imitates" the nature of the ultimate referent. And so

> The *junjuns*[1] break out in a wild *u*
> The *gongos*[2] resound with a deep *o*
> It is the Black race that undulates
> in a coarse rhythm. . . .

And thus the *Orfeo bongosero* provides the stimulus for the clanking excitement in the marches of Vachel Lindsay and Palés Matos, among others.

We see that the nature of the tema and its incarnation, the *Orfeo bongosero,* causes marked deviations from the esoterically oriented process of mythmaking in Gatsbian romance. Even in its corruption, *The Great Gatsby's* green light reaches back and forth, no matter how translucently, to an elevating Eden of nostalgic/futuristic dimensions. There thus might be stasis in present vulgarity, but that stasis impinges on a consciousness that the ashes of vulgarity need not be inevitable — and this, even as one accepts catastrophe as imminent.

The tom-toms or bongos of the tema negro do not generate this possibility for Palés Matos. Eden for the tema is "Tombuctú," a name, or more accurately, a sound which can only generate a centripetal force. At the center of its inward movement is the reduction of meaning or insight to percussion. The frequencies of the music that accompany and, indeed, embody the romance reach their climax in a coda that is quite properly a scherzo. That is part of the key. The predominance of the burlesque thus insists that the appropriate response to the tema negro inspiration conform to a perception of the Muse as Doggerel-Muse. Vulgarity as romance as myth gives way to vulgarity as romance as joke. All the refinements of poetic rhythm shed their complex permutations in the linear-simplicities of percussive slapstick.

Since profundity (thematic) is impossible there is little danger of that near-intolerable irony generated when a profound insight is wedded to inelegant form by a superior intelligence. The logical outcome in the Palés Matos school is not irony but a double descent into bathos. Thus, the majestic is conceived of in bathetic terms and resolved, as always, in what, within the limits of the creative process here, we may call jitanjáfora conceits. Thus, the centrifugal energy of the title "Black Majesty" stands in marked parody to its centripetal movement:

> Through the inflamed Antillean street
> walks Tembandumba of Quimbamba.[3]
> Flower of Tortola, rose of Uganda,
> For you, bombas and bambulas[4] crackle;
> For you, the West Indies burns its
> Nanigo[5] blood in wanton calendas.[6]
> Haiti offers you its calabashes;
> Jamaica gives you fiery rums;
> Cuba tells you: Get it, mulatta!
> And Puerto Rico: honey-colored, my amber!
>
> Up, my ghosts with black faces!
> Thunder, drums; shake, maracas.
> Through the inflamed Antillean street
> — Rumba, macumba, candombe, bambula[7] —
> walks Tembandumba of Quimbamba.

Thematic profundity may be impossible, but some modulation does take place within the tema negro usage. Palés Matos quite obviously transforms the neo-Freudian/neo-Hobbesian atavism of Eugene O'Neill's *Emperor Jones* into a kind of one-dimensional, primitivist infantilism. He achieves this by taking a somewhat cavalier attitude toward the psychological possibilities that the "darker registers" of primitivist exploration might offer. Whereas O'Neill explores the drama that lies in the tema negro's "desbordante alegría dionísiaca, . . . vago temblor de misterio," and "el ritmo congénito de la raza" (Rodríguez-Embil) played out as satanic, black mass, Palés Matos turns his attention elsewhere.

What he sees in "tierras rojas, islas de betún / Haití, Martinica, Congo, Camerún" his poetic devices simply cannot turn into anything but an exotic, "populist" *negrería fantasmal*. In O'Neill the darker registers impinge on a romance of demonic mythology, an attendant corollary, perhaps inevitable, of the tema negro. At a cruder level of metaphorical equivalents, Palés Matos plays Cecil B. DeMille to the tema negro, where O'Neill attempts the studied involutions of Ingmar Bergman.

In all this Palés Matos comes close but cannot quite match in sensitivity a near-contemporary primitivist, Henri Rousseau (Le Douanier), who, in painting, tended toward "botanical-garden boutiques [that] could never have existed, and whose sources for such scenes are very much in question" (Neville Weston, *The Reaches of Modern Art*). The potentially dynamic mana in the primitivist universe is reduced to an apparently naive, flat schema, defanging and freezing the animate and the inanimate in exotic stasis. In both Rousseau and Palés Matos there are, of course, no really fearful symmetries. It is perhaps subliminally possible to sense glimpses of a deeper purposiveness in Rousseau's canvases than in Palés Matos's elaborate jitanjáforas. The internal dynamics of Rousseau's frames suggest a centripetal *and* centrifugal movement that intimates a potentially surrealist logic — this, rather than the burlesque or bathos to which the apparently serious poems of Palés Matos descend, as in "Lament":

> The Black man is wretched
> from Havana to Zimbabue
> from Angola to Kanembu
> the Black man is wretched . . .
> He no longer dances his tu-cu-tu
> to the "adombe-ganga-monde"[8]

Even when the *mana* burns bright from a latent charge, it does so, in Palés Matos's poetry, in the context of a scherzo. The tema negro is red in tooth and nail in "Nam-Nam" but exists in a universe of romance that is Gothic-Farce:

Yum, yum. The fetishes open
their black mouths — yum, yum.
In the pupils of the witch doctor
a single flame — yum, yum.
The blood of the sacrifice
intoxicates the totem — yum, yum,
and Niggerland is all teeth
in the darkness — yum, yum.

Asia dreams its Nirvana.
America dances the jazz
Europe plays and theorizes
Africa grunts: yum, yum.

Miguel Enguídanos, in *La poesía de Luis Palés Matos,* approaches this
theme from a perspective that attributes intelligent intention ("Su vida se
le escapa en busca del sueño" — "His life escapes him in his search for the
dream") to this apparently dilettantish orchestration of the exotic. This is
escapist ("fantasmal") literature. It seeks in *la negrería,* among other
avenues,

the dream that is the natural state . . . where there are no clocks, nor
hours, nor days, nor weeks, nor somber faces, nor stuck-up gentlemen, nor
post offices, nor perfumed and haughty ladies: where the poet lives with
himself alone and with his dream of dreams: to be able to destroy the
time of mortals.

I see little need to quarrel with the sweeping protestations. The caveat is
in favor of reserving the idea of intelligent undertaking to the prototypical
"dreamers" in the literary and philosophical dialectic — such as "the
butterfly philosopher" Chuang Tzu or Calderón. In Palés Matos the dialectic resolves itself in vulgar romance, as facile as it perhaps might have
been inevitable.

There was, perhaps, much in the period that showed the routines of
reality with such intolerably crude immediacy that the escape into
romance was motivated more by reaction against that unacceptable reality.
This would explain, at least partly, the hyperbolic posturings in the escapist tendencies of the Twenties — whether we see the escape in the nearly
successful attempt in *Gatsby* (book and protagonist) to create ecstasy out
of that vast, meretricious beauty or in the cruder explosions of "populist"
fantasies in the tema negro of Palés Matos, Vachel Lindsay or Eugene
O'Neill. A corollary to this escapist "rage" is the equally hyperbolic
posture of those who chose confrontation rather than fantasy: Sinclair
Lewis raging in Zenith, Regino Pedroso in Cuba, D. H. Lawrence in England, Mencken, et al. The "rough beast," its hour come at last, slouches to

be born in the consciousness — and so unlooses mere anarchy.

It is interesting that the primitivist in the esoteric tradition of the Palés Matos school who does not quite incorporate the vulgar is Rousseau. Neville Weston elaborates,

> sometimes he painted from scenes that he knew well, but, more importantly, he worked from a mixture of memory and imagination, and so tapped the realms that surrealism was to reign over twenty years later. These exotic scenes — evocations of primeval forests which were a meeting-place for lions and tigers, botanically impossible flora, and voluptuous maidens — were magical, mysterious, and because of their improbability, essentially dreamlike.

It is also significant that Henri Rousseau died in 1910, and so did not live to see the murderous explosion of slaughter in World War I. That orgy of destruction, combined with earlier fin-de-siècle intimations of disaster, may have triggered a brutalization of the senses. The movement of history would seem, then, to confirm the rise and apparent immortality of an aristocracy of vulgarity. Nicolás Guillén is succinct and brutal and deliberately parodic in his statement of the case:

> Here are the servants of Mr. Babbitt.
> Those who educate their sons at West Point.
> Here are those who scream: "Hello, baby,"
> and smoke "Chesterfield" and "Lucky Strike."
> Here are the dancers of fox-trots,
> the boys of the jazz band. . . .

Hermann Hesse's near-ecstatic intimations of disaster after his glimpse into chaos *(Blick ins Chaos)* are rendered concrete in the dramatization of vulgarity that we see above in Guillén.

Already half of Europe, already at last half of Eastern Europe, on the way to Chaos, drives drunk in scared infatuation along the edge of the precipice, sings drunkenly, as though hymn singing, as Dmitri Karamazov sang. The offended bourgeois laughs at the songs; the saint and the seer hear them with tears.

It would be unfair to Palés Matos to suggest he was unaware of this sense of a waste or wasting land, where things fell apart. He is, and in "Pueblo" he shows he can respond with elegiac dignity:

> Have pity, Lord, have pity on my poor town
> where my poor people will die from nothing!
> That old notary who spends his days
> in his insignificant and slow rat's anxiety;

this obese magistrate with the huge empty belly
splashing about in his life as if in gravy;
that businessman — slow, even tempered, medieval;
these she-goats who frisk about in the sun's glare of the patio;
some beggar, some horse that crosses
— scabby, grey and skinny — these wide streets;
the cold and atrophying drowsiness of Sunday
playing billiards and cards in the casinos;
the whole, the whole boring flock of these lives
in this ancient town where nothing happens,
all this dies, falls, crumbles
by dint of being comfortable and at ease.
. . . . . .
    Have pity, Lord, pity on my poor town
where my poor people will die from nothing!

The age could not indefinitely and monotonously hold an elegiac pose. One consequence was Romance — in the context of a primitivist golden age, and against this the world of vulgar pretensions that so provoked Guillén. Some primitivists would turn the wasteland green:

He soon found himself disgusted with the mock Europe created by the colonials in the capital, Papeete, and, having once before escaped from being enslaved by money (when he left the Stock Exchange), he again threw off the restrictions of a normal life . . . enthusing over the wild landscape, the mysterious thickets, and the shaded brooks. The silence of the Polynesian night also excited him, and he said that it "hung there without even the sound of a bird; a falling leaf would not destroy the silence, but would appear like the rustling of spirits."

In this respect, Paul Gauguin is a kindred spirit to Rousseau.

    In the Nineteen-Twenties, the tema negro would have some primitivists consider that the rhythm of life was a jazz or rumba rhythm. It was a period, says Langston Hughes, when "a large and enthusiastic number of people were crazy about Negroes." In the hands of a gifted artist, neither perception nor delicacy were sacrificed to a craze. Palés Matos and his fellow-travelers approached the craze from an essentially vulgar direction — and then proceeded to incorporate that vulgarity in the romance that resulted.

    Come, brothers, to the celebration.
Dance the dance of the Black god
around the bonfire
where the white prisoner burns.
Let the most beautiful maiden
tear her flesh and open her sex,
so that the manliest of the warriors
can enter, impregnating her.

. . . . .
The gongo-drum resounds in the silence . . .
Bass drum of the Congo, great Mongo,[9]
The bass drum of the Congo is content.

The abrupt, open-thighed vision of sexuality in the above lines takes place and is consummated in the workman-like rhythms of Palés Matos's style. In a certain sense, therefore, the perspective on sexuality in his tema negro primitivism is exotic-voyeuristic rather than dynamic-purposive — and this, in spite of the "Para que pase, fecundándola / El más viril de los guerreros." We do not have here a set scene whose import is essentially an attempt to develop a prophetic vision of primitivist, moral glamor, basing that glamor on the ecstasy and procreativity of the power below the navel. For that kind of response we have to turn to another primitivist, D. H. Lawrence, whose *Lady Chatterley's Lover* was published c. 1925, thus coinciding neatly with Palés Matos at the height of his interest in the tema negro.

While *The Great Gatsby* maintains sexual stasis in a kind of titillatingly ascetic eroticism, D. H. Lawrence transforms stasis into emphatically primitivist kinesis. This is evident in the poems that linger with sometimes clinical but decidedly caressing interest in copulating animals. It, of course, reaches its climax in those typically Lawrencian, polyphonic cadences which fuse physical, emotional and psychic ecstasy in a romance of the orgasmic moment. Here, and to a grosser extent in Palés Matos, lies the modern equivalent of Erich Auerbach's observation in *Mimesis: The Representation of Reality in Western Literature:*

The romance, finally, *fabula milesiaca* is . . . so crammed with magic, adventure, and mythology, so overburdened with erotic detail, that it cannot possibly be considered an imitation of everyday life as it existed at the time — quite apart from the unrealistic and rhetorical stylization of its language.

Palés Matos shares the same universe but at a somewhat lower level — in the magico-comic stratum, in "las papiamentosas antillas" and "las patualesas islas."

Not that modulation of the sexual is absent in Palés Matos. The kind of sexuality whose principal agent is the *Orfeo bongosero* manifests itself in percussive performances which have as much lyricism as unmodulated drum beats can have — which is to say, none. There clearly are intimations of a Dionysiac energy "en el silencio de la selva" where "el gran negro baila poseído / De la gran bestia original." But they remain mere intimations of the Dionysiac, since the *locus* of their possible incarnation, the poet's architecture, is built on devices that discompose the Dionysiac into the *farcical.* "Numen" thus finds its cornerstone in the repeated jitanjáfora sequence

> Jungla africana — Tembandumba
> Maniqua haitiana — Macandal.

Despite their lexical values, the repetition of these sounds soon strips them of meaning, reducing them to rhythmic quantities with the prescribed tema negro resonance.

Nonetheless, sexuality becomes a more generalized ambience of turgid eroticism when the *Negra* is principal. And this is so even when that eroticism is localized in the predictable tema negro sounds: "Mussumba, Tombuctú, Faranfangana." In "Pueblo Negro" the primitivist universe heaves and pulsates with "la luz rabiosa," "la humedad del árbol corpulento," "lodo suculento," and "guturaciones alargadas." At the center of this succulent and equatorially exotic heat lies the Negress — tumescent with "un canto monorítmico . . . / Pululado de ues."

> It is the Black woman who sings
> . . . . .
> the Black woman of the sun-lit regions
> who smells of earth, of wild beast, of sex.
> It is the Black woman who sings,
> and her passionate song spreads
> like a clear day of bliss
> beneath the shade of coconut palms.

In the final analysis, where Wordsworth dissolves the reality of his Solitary Reaper, "yon highland lass," in the evanescent mysticism of his primitivist universe, Palés Matos here locates the *Negra* in the seduction of the word "sexo," which ends "Pueblo Negro."

> At the sound of her song
> everything is silenced
> and the only thing left in my soul
> is the deep *u* of the wild dipthong
> in whose maternal curve is hidden
> the prolific harmony of the sex.

If we accept the stylistic truism that melodramatic poses maintained in melodramatically exaggerated structures result in the disintegration of apparent order into chaos (farce), then a certain measure of irony lies at the heart of Palés Matos's escapist fantasy. And this is all the more so because the melodramatic fecundity of this *topografía negra* stands in marked stylistic and emotional contrast to a universe of sterility which, in "Topografía," he captures with a bitter and near-clipped lucidity that recalls T. S. Eliot's response to the arid landscape of "The Hollow Men" (1922):

> This is the sterile, unpleasant land
> where the cactus sprouts.
> Whitish saltpeter bed that
> the bird, pierced with thirst, crosses.
> With dry salt marshes, spaced
> at wide intervals,
> and a fixed sky, unchangeable and mute,
> covering the whole circumference.
>
> . . . . .
> This is my whole history:
> salt, aridity, weariness,
> a motionless fixedness of the swamp,
> and a cry, there in the depths,
> like a terrible, stubborn mushroom
> coagulating among spongy carnations
> of useless, spent dreams.

These "thoughts of a dry brain" (Eliot) in a dry season give way to the orchestration of fertility symbols in the *topografía negra* we have just examined. T. S. Eliot resolves his confrontation with aridity in the penitential litanies of Ash Wednesday: sterility is replaced by anticipated fertility in the "blue / green" seasons of the Virgin Mary. D. H. Lawrence, as noted before, resolves his hysterical hostility against a "civilization of steel, coal and iron" and against a "beastly bourgeoisie" in the melodrama of sexual ecstasy and mysticism — be it in Jesus ("The Man Who Died") or the Gamekeeper *(Lady Chatterly's Lover).*

The nature of the trivialization of Palés Matos's response in this matter may better be understood if we place the Virgin Mary, Jesus and the Gamekeeper in analogous reference to *The Great Gatsby*'s Green Light — and then, if we place all these referents in opposition to the tema negro (in its Negress or *Orfeo bongosero* manifestation). The Green Light illuminates alternative visions which maintain an intra-Western ethical and esthetic relevance — if not decorum. The dynamics of their exploration is not voyeurism (or mere "slumming") in a universe whose energies are not easily brought into the cultural continuum of the West. In essence, the "slumming explorer" clearly seeks no permanent residence. The "alternative" is merely the temporarily titillating. It is reduced to its most skeletally accessible dimensions mainly because the dilettante explorer exists (or perhaps merely *wishes* to exist) in an eternal present. Emilio Ballagas states the case with succinct clarity when he talks of "una expresión turística en el tiempo y el espacio, sin dimensión histórica." Of the other Twenties fantasists mentioned, D. H. Lawrence comes closest to the pose adopted by Palés Matos. I refer specifically to the sexual "slumming" that allows Lawrence to make of the gamekeeper his Phallic Messiah. But in Lawrence the dialectic is in a class rather than a race differential.

In non-fictional terms, and at a somewhat Gatsbian level of actual society, the "scream of salutation" that spread through the Théatre des Champs-Elysees at the sight of Josephine Baker may be seen as the actualized equivalent of Palés Matos's jitanjáfora excitements in his *topografía negra*. The year is 1925:

She made her entry entirely nude except for a pink flamingo feather between her limbs; she was being carried upside down and doing the split on the shoulder of a black giant. Midstage he paused, and with his long fingers holding her basket-wise around the waist, swung her in a slow cartwheel to the stage floor, where she stood, like his magnificent discarded burden, in an instance of complete silence. She was an unforgettable female ebony statue. A scream of salutation spread through the theater.

So writes Janet Flanner in *Paris was Yesterday* (1925–1939). Josephine Baker left her audience "hungry for further fantastic truths. . . . Most of Paris who had seen the opening night went back for the next two or three nights as well; they were never twice alike." And

Somewhere along the development, either then or it might have been a year or so later, as Josephine's career ripened, she appeared with her famous festoon of bananas worn like a savage skirt around her hips.

And one is reminded of precisely the level at which Palés Matos made contact

It is the Black woman who sings
. . . . .
the Black woman of the sun-lit regions
who smells of earth, of wild beast, of sex.

Vulgarity and hedonism meet in a universe of romance, but that triadic movement may be seen as an attempt to create an escapist haven out of the very attributes which had created (and were still creating) a world whose "vast carelessness" *(Gatsby)* had bruised "Miedo. Desolación. Asfixia. / . . . Sal, aridez, cansancio" ("Topografía") into the sensibility. Federico de Onís suggests as much:

Palés is the product of bitter, ironic post-Modernism who finally discovered a new direction in interpretation. Bitter and ironic also was the Negro side of the Antillean soul.

Tomás Blanco so quotes him in *Sobre Palés Matos*.

Primitivism in these years thus occupies a temporal and spatial oasis of desperate vulgarity between the "unmentionable odor of death" of World War I and World War II. The irreducible distillate upon which the perception of reality depends is clearly stated in the opening paragraph of *Lady Chatterly's Lover* – *the* catastrophe (World War I) had happened. And yet, by 1939,

the Louvre and other state museums are closed; the art treasures are being shipped off to the provinces. As art objects, the palace of Fontainebleau and Versailles are also closed, but unfortunately they can't be moved. The American Hospital at Neuilly is packed and ready to be transferred to Etretat, near Havre, at the zero hour. While Poland's citizens have been urged to buy a hundred and fifty pounds of potatoes, flour, etc., the French are being asked not to hoard.

Janet Flanner's canvas is international. In his intermittent returns from his *negreria fantasmal*, Palés Matos translates the vision into microcosmic landscapes. In "Lullaby," the last poem in *Tuntún de pasa y griferia*, narcotization is attempted with self-mesmerising and self-caressing imperatives:

> My soul, my poor soul!
> There are the monstrous butchers.
> Pass stealthily, scarcely touching
> these lands cursed with silence;
> from the great green silence
> that coagulates its thick humor in the caverns
> and beneath the moon in the tragedies
> of distant, illusory shipwrecks.
>
> My soul, my poor soul!
> Above your ancient theme
> these fields cross, softly,
> in order not to wake a proper dream.

The use of the tema negro in the Twenties thus fits into the mosaic of apocalyptic visions and "vast carelessness." Langston Hughes, writing out of the Harlem of 1928, translates his perception into the epigrammatic clarity of "Lenox Avenue: Midnight":

The rhythm of life
Is a jazz rhythm,
Honey.
The gods are laughing at us.

NOTES

1. *junjuns:* a kind of primitive violin.
2. *gongos:* a type of drum.
3. *Tembandumba of Quimbamba:* An African queen (symbolizing the Black woman) of an ancient and remote kingdom.
4. *bomba:* Large drum; *bambula:* Puerto Rican dance.
5. *Nanigo:* A secret society of Blacks which venerates ancestors.
6. *calenda:* Dance of African origin.
7. *Rumba . . . bambula:* Dances of African origin.
8. *"adombe . . . monde":* An African phrase used to invoke the gods.
9. *Mongo:* jungle god.

ANN VENTURE YOUNG

The Black Woman in Afro-Caribbean Poetry

> With the equatorial circle
> cinched to her waist as if to a small world
> the Black woman, a new woman
> advances in her sheer robe of a serpent.
> — Nicolás Guillén, "New Woman"

Even a cursory investigation of the poetry variously referred to as *negrista, mulata, negroide, negra, afroamericana,* and *afroantillana* reveals the preoccupation of the poets of this genre with the Afro-American woman, the *negra* and more often the *mulata.* Titles such as "Bailadora de rumba" by the Cuban Ramón Guirao, Nicolás Guillén's "Mulata," Emilio Ballagas's "Elegía de María Belén Chacón," "Mulata-Antilla" by the Puerto Rican poet Luis Palés Matos, and the Mexican José Juan Tablada's "Canción de la mulata," abound in poetry written during the 1930s, the apogee of the negrista movement in Latin American and Caribbean letters.

What is the investigator's initial impression, hardly more than an intuition, of the centrality of the Black woman in the poetic production of this era is firmly supported by the research and investigations of an ever-increasing band of scholars and critics who are now contributing at an unprecedented rate to the heretofore scanty data available about the negrista movement in Latin America and the Caribbean. There is mounting evidence to the effect that, whereas the Thirties represent the high point of literary creativity in this mode, the Seventies will be characterized as the period of the renaissance, if not the nascence, of scholarly activity and productivity in this field.

The present decade is witnessing a concerted and dedicated effort to penetrate into the presence and meaning of the Black experience in Latin America and of its translation, faithful or not, into the poetry of the region. This is the period of inquiry into the complexities of that experience in the Americas. More, it is a time of reevaluation and reassessment, a time of de-mystification, a time for dispelling old myths and perhaps for creating new ones. It is a time of image shattering and image building, a

137

time when Black people are participating in the evaluative and formulative process to a greater extent than ever before. Blacks are no longer content to have their experiences defined exclusively by others; they now insist upon defining their own unique and substantial contribution to the cultural development of the Western world.

Further, the Afro-American is reaffirming his cultural and spiritual bonds with Africa and with its descendants throughout the world. He is awakening to the historical realities of his oppression and casting off the elaborate chains which had been designed not only to immobilize him physically and demoralize him spiritually, but also to separate him culturally from his kin, the other branches of the giant baobab tree. He is on the move, from Harlem and Loiza Aldea to Barlovento, Cali, Esmeraldas and beyond, forging another chain, this one built of brotherhood, knowledge and freedom.

The critic and the poet, unwittingly or not, often emulate the oppressive strategy of dividing and thereby lessening the numerical strength of Blacks. Traditionally, one such division has been based on depth of skin color: mulatto, colored, octaroon, quadroon, and black. But because even this color coding system so often lacks precision, especially for the poet, preference is given in this article to the use of the terms "Black" and "Afro-American" in designating the "new woman" in Afro-Hispanic poetry. For it is not so much her skin tone which is the determinant but rather her participation in a process of acculturation which makes her unique. It is no doubt significant that this process of acculturation in Latin America and the Caribbean began only a few years after the "discovery" and colonization of the New World by the Spanish and Portuguese. Thus, the African slave woman was in a position from the very onset to insinuate the richness of her cultural heritage into the lifestyle of the emerging colonies. She had brought to that alien land much more than her physical self; she was a repository of philosophies, languages, religious beliefs and rituals, music, and dance forms. It was with these gifts that she endowed and enriched the New World.

It is from this rich store of historical data that the negrista poets might have discovered the cultural authenticity of the Black woman, but unfortunately they have elected almost unanimously to highlight her physical attributes, her sensuality, a choice which reveals more about the poet than about his subject. And in so doing, they are continuing a tradition that has clear antecedents in the tenth-century literature of the Iberian Peninsula, which precedes by almost two hundred years the first known work written in the Castilian language. This is a tradition in which pejorative allusions to the color black already exist. In this peninsular literature, with rare exceptions, the Black woman is depicted as an inferior being, a symbol of sensuality and evil.

The poetry of the negrista movement reflects this pejorative attitude toward the Black woman, while the poet seems to recognize her importance in American life. He manifests in his works an almost irresistible attraction to her; he portrays her largely as a superstitious, hip-swaying high priestess of sensuality.

Unlike the Euro-American woman, an object of adoration, whose beauty in poetic tradition is often likened to that of the flower, the Afro-American woman has inspired a different kind of imagery. She is rarely the flower of the land, but rather the fruit *(caimito, aguacate, mamey, guanábana)* and vegetable *(frijol, yuca, boniato)*. She is the cane field and its products – *melaza, caña azúcar.* She symbolizes the African dance – *la rumba, el son, el danzón* – and she is the instrument which accompanies the dance *(maracas, tambor, bongó)*. She is the serpent and the temptress. For some poets, she is also the homeland.

Earlier poets are obsessed with the physical attributes of the Afro-American woman. This preoccupation is perhaps born of their inability or refusal to conceive of her in terms which accord her full human status. She is perceived from without and seems to represent just another element in the tropical environment. There is an almost total disregard for an essence which might transcend the color of her skin and the rotundity of her buttocks.

The "fruit imagery," as G. R. Coulthard calls it in the chapter "The Coloured Woman in Caribbean Poetry" in his *Race and Colour in Caribbean Literature,* is typical of the vehicle used for the presentation of this superficial view of the woman. The fruits of a land are cultivated not for their beauty, but rather to fulfill a more utilitarian function, that of nourishing and sustaining the consumer. The fruit, so that it might perform its duty, is variously handled, savoured, squeezed, and devoured. Mansour asserts that by means of "fruit imagery" the poets successfully capture the colors, movements, odors, textures and forms characteristic of the Afro-American woman.[1] She continues by noting that the tropical landscape and all of its elements converge in the woman's sensuality. It must be remembered, however, that the poets are most often expressing what they consider to be the Black woman's excessive sensuality and primitivism.

José Juan Tablada's Black woman expresses these sentiments in "Canción de la mulata":

> my body is a nocturnal garden;
> my breasts two guanabanas

For Luis Palés Matos, she is the personification of the Antilles:

Here in its green dress is the guanabana
with its delicate and soft panties
of muslin; here is the star apple
with its childish milk; here is the pineapple
with its soprano crown. . . . All
these fruits, oh mulatta, you offer to me
in the clear bay of your body
browned by the suns of the tropics.[2]

Other imagery is employed to describe the extreme, almost animal-like sensuality which the poet attributes to the woman of African descent. She provokes comparisons with many elements which are native to the tropical setting, particularly images related to the production of sugar — *melaza* (molasses), *guarapo* (juice of the sugar cane), *ron* (rum), *cachaza* (rum). Such imagery reinforces the notion of the Black woman's centrality to and inseparability from the tropical landscape; indeed, historically, she has made important cultural and economic contributions to the development of the land. Both the fruit imagery and other symbols relating to sugar and its production underscore the expendable nature of the Black woman. She is one more natural resource, sought after, cultivated, and exploited for the pleasure and satisfaction of the "master." In Nicolás Guillén's "Secuestro de la mujer de Antonio," the aggressive protagonist who wants Antonio's woman for himself says:

I am going to gulp you down,
like a drink of rum;
I am going to pour you into the cup
of a song
From here you will not go, mulata,
to the market or to your house;
here will grind your buttocks
the cane harvest of your sweat. . . .

Another example of gross sensuality in the portrayal of the Black woman is to be found in this fragment from Luis Palés Matos's "Black Majesty":

Swinging her hips the queen approaches
and from her immense rump glide
provocative wiggles which the drum converts
into rivers of sugar and molasses.
Black mill of sensuous sugar cane,
the hips, mass on mass,
squeeze out rhythms, exuding sweat,
and the grinding ends in a dance.

The Spaniard, Alfonso Camín, who spent many years in the Americas, especially in Cuba, and who is considered one of the early negrista poets, portrays the Afro-American woman in his "Elogio de la negra":

> Black woman, twin vigor of a race
> made of honey, of lust and rum,
> mixture of yucca and sweet potato,
> of coffee and brown sugar.

Another symbol that is frequently employed in the poetic description of the Black woman is that of the snake. Many poets compare her movements with those of the serpent; she is the creature of sinuous and slithering gyrations, tantalizing the male. Other poets, influenced, no doubt, by the biblical fable, view the snake and the Afro-American woman as evil despoilers of all that is good in man. Francisco Muñóz del Monte synthesizes these two somewhat different views in his poem, "La mulata."

> The genteel mulata then seizes him
> convulsive, frenetic, desirous,
> and in a voluptuous murmuring coo
> her mouth exhales the word love.

> And she triumphs as she speaks. The man is hers,
> the white man obeys her slavishly;
> in the fatal mouth of the serpent
> the proud bird fell.

> . . . . .

> Agile snake, hungry boa,
> the mulata her victim subdues,
> she oppresses, stretches, squeezes, confounds, grips him,
> and sucks, and licks, and bites his furor.

As American as it is African, the snake is a mysterious, erotic and totemic animal which preys on the defenseless bird, often a white bird. In Afro-Caribbean poetry the Black woman personifies this ferocious animal of prey, who ensnares its victim and devours it.

The Afro-American woman is also portrayed as a dancer who gyrates to music of African origin; accompanied by percussive instruments, she dances the *son, danzón, rumba,* and *guateque.* Almost every negrista poet has been intrigued by the violent movements of the Black woman. José Z. Tallet's "La rumba," which was included in the repertoire of the popular *recitadora* Berta Singerman, presents this portrait of the plasticity of the "Negra Tomasa."

> The powerful buttocks of Tomasa
> around an invisible axis,
> like an arrow revolve with fury,
> challenging with rhythmic, lubricious abandon
> the salacious attack of Che Encarnación. . . .

For the Cuban José Sánchez-Boudy, the Afro-American woman typifies the rhythm and essence of the dance. Implicit in the narrator's exhortation to the dancer is the idea that she alone gives full life and meaning to the dance.

> Mulata, give me your flavor,
> for beating my drum,
> Of rum and palm tree,
> of guayabera and sound.

Even the absent dancer, who may be too old to dance, or dead, like Emilio Ballagas's María Belén Chacón, or missing from the festivities, like Marcelino Arozarena's "Caridá," holds sway over her admirer. So renowned and powerful is the artistry of the dancer that the protagonist retains a vivid mental picture of her rhythmic movements.

> María Belén Chacón, María Belén Chacón.
> María Belén, María Belén;
> with your buttocks swinging,
> from Camagüey to Santiago . . .
> from Santiago to Camagüey.

Marcelino Arozarena wonders:

> Why does the daughter of Iemayá not come to the feast,
> the fleshy,
> the pompous,
> the happy and mischievous Caridá?

Although we have concluded with a fragment from "Caridá," Arozarena's work, like that of Nicolás Guillén, is devoid of what Janheinz Jahn calls "descriptive exoticism." These two Cuban poets go far beyond the portrayal of the Afro-American woman as a primitive sensual creature. They seem to know that while she is the embodiment of much that is central to life in the land of the "cross and the drum" — the fauna, the flora, the rhythm — that she is much more. Indeed, she is worthy of further exploration by students of Latin American and Caribbean literature.

NOTES

1. Monica Mansour, *La poesía negrista* (México: Ediciones Era, 1973), p.181.
2. Luis Palés Matos, *Poesía 1915-1956* (San Juan: Editorial, U.P.R., 1968), p. 2.

MIRIAM DeCOSTA

Selected Bibliography

POETRY

Arozarena, Marcelino. *Canción negra sin color*. Havana, 1966.
Auque Lara, Jaimer. *A-fraía, poemas negristas*. Colombia, 1964.
Ballagas, Emilio. *Antología de poesía negra hispanoamericana*. Madrid, 1935.
———. *Cuaderno de poesía negra*. Santa Clara, 1934.
———. *Mapa de la poesía negra*. Buenos Aires, 1947.
———. *Obra poética*. Miami: Mnemosyne Publishing, Inc., 1969.
———. *Orbita de Emilio Ballagas*. Edited by Rosario Antuña. Havana, 1965.
Barrios, Pilar. *Campo afuera*. Montevideo, 1958.
———. *Mis cantos (poesía)*. Montevideo: García, 1949.
———. *Nuestra raza*. Montevideo, 1947.
———. *Piel negra (poesías 1917–1947)*. Montevideo: García, 1947.
Brindis de Salas, Virginia. *Cien cárceles de amor*. Montevideo, 1949.
———. *Pregón de Marimorena*. Montevideo, 1946.
Cabral, Manuel del. *Doce poemas negros*. Ciudad Trujillo, 1935.
———. *Trópico negro*. Buenos Aires, 1941.
Caignet, Félix B. *A golpe de maracas, poemas negros en papel mulato*. Havana, 1950.
Calcanó, Francisco. *Poetas de color*. Havana, 1887.
Candelario Obeso, Nicolás Guillén, Jorge Artel y otros poetas negristas: sus mejores versos. Bogota: Editorial La Gran Colombia n. d.
Cuero, Orlando Tenorio. *Desde atrás de la vida* n. d.
Devieri, Hugo. *Versos de piel morena*. Buenos Aires, 1945.
Echevarría, Colón. *Tambor de negros*. Buenos Aires: Editorial Norte, 1946.
Estupiñán Bass, Nelson. *Canto negro por la luz: poemas para negros y blancos*. Editorial Rumiñahui, 1954.

———. *Timarán y Cuabú: cuaderno de poesía para el pueblo.* Quito: Editorial Casa de la Cultura Ecuatoriana, 1956.

Guillén, Nicolás. *Balada.* Havana: Empresa Consolidada de Artes Gráficas, 1962.

———. *Cantos para soldados y sones para turistas.* Mexico: Editorial Masas, 1937.

———. *Cuba libre: poems.* Trans. by Langston Hughes and Ben F. Carruthers. Los Angeles, 1961.

———. *Motivos de son.* Havana: Imprenta Rambla Bouza, 1930.

———. *La paloma de vuelo popular.* Buenos Aires: Losada, 1958.

———. *Patria o Muerte! The Great Zoo and Other Poems.* Edited and translated by Robert Márquez. New York: Monthly Review Press, 1972.

———. *Poemas de amor.* Havana: Cuadernos de Poesía 6, 1964.

———. *El son entero; suma poética (1929-1946).* Buenos Aires: Pleamar, 1947.

———. *La rueda dentada.* Havana: Inst. Cub. del Libro, 1972.

———. *Sóngoro Cosongo. Poemas mulatos.* Havana: Ucar García, 1931.

———. *Tengo.* Havana: Universidad Central de Las Villas, 1964.

———. *West Indies, Ltd.* Havana: Ucar García, 1934.

Guirao, Ramón. *Antología de la poesía afrocubana.* 1928.

———. *Orbita de la poesía afrocubana, 1928-37.* Havana, 1939.

Lanuza, José Luis. "Cancionero de negros," *Coplas y cantares argentinos.* Buenos Aires: Emecé Editores, S.A., 1952.

Latino, Simón. *Antología de la poesía negra.* Buenos Aires: Cuadernillos de Poesía, 1963.

———. *Los mejores versos de la poesía negra.* Buenos Aires, 1956.

———. *Los versos mejores de Nicolás Guillén.* Buenos Aires: Editorial Nuestra América, 1961.

León, Nicolás. *El negrito poeta mexicano y sus populares versos.* Mexico: Impresora del Museo Nacional, 1912.

López Albújar, Enrique. *De la tierra brava: poemas afroyungas.* Lima, 1938.

Manzano, Juan Francisco. *Cantos a Lesbia.* Havana, 1821.

———. *Poems by a Slave in the Island of Cuba.* Trans. by R. R. Madden, 1840.

Marquéz, Robert, and David A. McMurray. *Man-Making Words: Selected Poems of Nicolás Guillén.* Amherst: Univ. of Mass. Press, 1972.

Martán Góngora, Helcías. "Mester de negrería," *Suma poética: 1963-1968.* Bogota: Biblioteca del Instituto Colombiano de Cultura Hispánica, 1969, pp. 117–152.

Ortiz, Adalberto. *El animal herido.* Quito, 1959.

———. *Tierra, son y tambor: cantares negros y mulatos.* Mexico, 1945.

Palés Matos, Luis. *Poesía (1915-1956).* Introd. by Federico de Onis. San Juan, 1957.

———. *Tuntún de pasa y grifería.* San Juan, 1950.

Pedroso, Regino. *Antología poética.* Havana, 1939.

———. *Más allá canta el mar.* Havana, 1939.

———. *Poemas: antología.* Havana, 1966.

Pereda Valdés, Ildefonso. *Antología de la poesía negra americana.* Montevideo: Organización Medina, 1953.

————. *Cancionero popular uruguayo*. Montevideo, 1947.

————. *La guitarra de los negros*. Montevideo: Editoriales La Cruz del Sur y Martín Fierro, n. d.

————. *Raza negra*. Montevideo, 1929.

Preciado, Antonio. *Tal como somos*. Quito, 1959.

Ruiz del Vizo, Hortensia. *Black Poetry of the Americas*. Miami: Ediciones Universal, 1972.

————. *Poesía negra del Caribe y otras áreas*. Miami: Ediciones Universal, 1972.

Santa Cruz, Nicomedes. *Antología: décimas y poemas*. Lima: Campondónico, 1971.

————. *Canto a mi Perú*. Lima: Librería Studium, 1966.

————. *Cumanana*. Lima: Librería Juan Mejía Baca, 1964.

————. *Décimas*. Lima: Librería Studium, 1966.

————. *Ritmos negros del Perú*. Buenos Aires: Editorial Losada, S.A., 1971.

Sanz y Díaz, José. *Lira negra*. Madrid: Aguilar, S.A., 1945.

Toruño, Juan Felipe. *Poesía negra: ensayo, antología*. Mexico: Colección Obsidiana, 1953.

Valdés, Gabriel de la Concepción. *Poesías de Plácido*. Mexico, 1904.

————. *Poesías selectas de Plácido*. Havana, 1930.

Valdés-Cruz, Rosa. *La poesía negroide en América*. New York: Las Américas, 1970.

Vianello, Raúl C. *Versos negros*. Mexico: Editora Continental, 1942.

DRAMA

Calderón de la Barca, Pedro. *Los hijos de la fortuna: Teágenes y Cariclea* in *Biblioteca de Autores Españoles*, Vol. XII. Madrid, 1926, pp. 87–110.

————. *Sabila del oriente y gran reina de Sabá*.

Claramonte, Andrés de. *El valiente negro en Flandes* in *Biblioteca de Autores Españoles*, Vol. XLIII. Madrid, 1857, pp. 491–509.

Lope de Rueda. *Obras*, II. Edic. de la Real Academia Española. Madrid, 1909, pp. 76–85, 101–107, 178–87.

Quiñones de Benavente, Luis. "El negrito hablador y sin color anda la niña," *Entremeses, loas y jácaras*, Vol. II. Edited by Cayetano Rosell. Madrid, 1874, pp. 29–39.

Vega Carpio, Lope Felix de. *El mayor rey de los reyes* in *Obras de Lope de Vega*. Madrid, 1929.

————. *Nacimiento de Cristo* in *Obras de Lope de Vega*. Madrid, 1929.

————. *El negro del mejor amo* in *Obras de Lope de Vega*, Vol. XI. Madrid, 1929, pp. 66–98.

————. *La vitoria de la honra* in *Obras de Lope de Vega*. Madrid, 1929.

Ximénez de Enciso, Diego. *El encubierto y Juan Latino*. Edited by Eduardo Julia Martínez. Madrid, 1951, pp. vii–lxxii, 141–356.

NARRATIVES

Barnet, Miguel. *Biografía de un cimarrón*. Mexico: Colección Mínima, Siglo XX Editores.

Cabrera, Lydia. *Cuentos de Jicotea*. Miami, 1971.

——. *Cuentos negros de Cuba*. Havana, 1940.

——. *Porqué . . . cuentos negros de Cuba*. 1948.

Cyrus, Stanley. *El cuento negrista sudamericano: antología*. Quito: Editorial Casa de la Cultura Ecuatoriana, 1973.

Díaz Sánchez. *Cam: ensayo sobre el negro*. Maracaibo, 1932.

Díaz Sánchez, Ramón. *La Virgen no tiene cara y otros cuentos*. Buenos Aires, 1951.

Diez Canseco, José. *Estampas mulatas*. Lima: Populibros Peruanos, 1940.

——. *Lima: coplas y guitarras*. Lima, 1949.

Franco, José L. *Autobiografía, cartas y versos de Juan Manzano*. Havana, 1937.

Guirao, Ramón. *Cuentos y leyendas negros de Cuba*. Havana: Ediciones "Mirador," 1942.

Lachatañeré, Rómulo. *Oh, mío Yamayá! cuentos*. Manzanillo, Cuba, 1938.

López Albújar. *De mi casona*. Lima: Librería Editorial, 1966.

——. *Los caballeros del delito. estudio criminológico del bandolerismo en algunos departamentos del Perú*. Lima: Compañia de Impresiones y Publicidad, 1936.

——. *Memorias*. Lima: Talleres Gráficos P. L. Villanueva, S.A., 1963.

Manzano, Juan Francisco. *Autobiografía, cartas y versos*. Estudio preliminar de José L. Franco. Havana, 1937.

Ortiz, Adalberto. *La entundada*. Quito, Ecuador: Editorial Casa de la Cultura Ecuatoriana, 1971.

Truque, Carlos Arturo. *El día que terminó el verano y otros cuentos*. Bogota: Instituto Colombiano de Cultura, 1973.

Zapata Olivella, Manuel. *Cuentos de muerte y libertad*. Bogota: Colección Narradores Colombianos de Hoy, 1961.

——. *Pasión vagabunda (relatos)*. Bogota: Editorial Santafé, 1949.

——. *¿Quién dio el fusil a Oswald? y otros cuentos*. Bogota: Editorial Revista Colombiana, 1967.

NOVELS

Avellaneda, Gertrudis Gómez de. *Sab*. Salamanca: Ediciones Anaya, S.A., 1970.

Carpentier, Alejo. *Ecué-Yamba-O*. Madrid, 1933.

Díaz Sánchez, Ramón. *Cumboto*. Barcelona: Circulo de Autores, 1972.

——. *Mene*. Caracas, 1969.

Estupiñán Bass. Nelson. *Cuando los guayacanes florecían*. Quito: Editorial Casa de la Cultura Ecuatoriana, 1954.

——. *El paraíso*. Quito: Editorial Casa de la Cultura Ecuatoriana, 1958.

——. *El último río*. Quito: Editorial Casa de la Cultura Ecuatoriana, 1966.

Gallegos, Romulo. *Pobre negro*. Buenos Aires: Austral, 1970.

Gilbert, Enrique Gil. *El negro Santander*. Guayaquil, Ecuador, 1968.

Hernández Franco, Tomás. *Yelidá*. Ciudad Trujillo, 1942.

López Albujar, Enrique. *Matalaché*. Lima: Juan Mejia Baca, 1928.

Mora Serrano, Manuel. *Juego de dominó*. Santo Domingo: Ediciones de Taller, 1973.

Morúa Delgado, Martín. *La familia Unzúazu*. Havana: Edición de la Comisión del Centenario de M. Morúa Delgado, 1957.

————. *Sofía*. Havana: Edición de la Comisión del Centenario de M. Morúa Delgado, 1957.

Novás Calvo, Lino. *El negrero*. Buenos Aires: Espasa-Calpe, 1944.

Ortiz, Adalberto. *Camino y puerto de la angustia*. Mexico, 1945.

————. *El espejo y la ventana*. Guayaquil, Ecuador, 1970.

————. *Juyungo, historia de un negro, una isla y otros negros*. Navarra, Spain: Salvat Editores, S.A., 1971.

————. *La mala espalda*. Guayaquil, 1952.

Palacios, Arnaldo. *Las estrellas son negras*. Bogota: Editorial Revista Colombiana, 1971.

Suárez y Romero, Anselmo. *Francisco*. Havana, 1947.

Villaverde, Cirilo. *Cecilia Valdés*. New York: Las Americas, 1964.

Zambrana, Antonio. *El negro Francisco; novela de costumbres cubanas*. Havana, 1951.

Zapata Olivella, Manuel. *La calle 10*. Bogota: Ediciones "Casa de la Cultura," n. d.

————. *Chambacú: corral de negros*. Medellín: Editorial Bedout, 1967.

————. *Detrás del rostro*. Madrid: Aguilar, 1963.

————. *En Chimá nace un santo*. Barcelona: Seix Barral, 1964.

————. *El grito de la independencia*. Cartagena, Colombia: Impr. Departamental de Bolivar, 1961.

————. *He visto la noche*. San Rafael: Impr. Nacional de Cuba, 1962.

————. *Hotel de vagabundos*. Bogota: Ediciones Espiral, 1955.

————. *Tierra mojada*.

CRITICAL STUDIES

Allen, Alma. "Literary Relations Between Spain and Africa," *The Journal of Negro History* (April, 1965).

Arrom, José Juan. "La poesía afrocubana," *Revista Iboamericana* (Feb. 1942), 379–411.

————. "Presencia del negro en la poesía folklórica americana," *Certidumbre de América*. Havana, 1959, 83–116.

Augier, Angel. "The Cuban Poetry of Nicolás Guillén." Translated by Joseph M. Bernstein. *Phylon*, 7, No. 1 (1951), 29–36.

Cabral, Manuel del. "Poesía negra," *Revista Dominicana de Cultura*, 1, No. 2 (Dec., 1955), 223–226.

Castellano, Juan R. "El negro esclavo en el entremés del Siglo de Oro," *Hispania* (March, 1961), 55–65.

Chasca, Edmond de. "The Phonology of the Speech of the Negroes in Early Spanish Drama," *HR*, 14 (1946), 322–329.

148 / SELECTED BIBLIOGRAPHY

Cobb, Martha. "Africa in Latin America: Customs, Culture, Literature," *Black World*, 21 (Aug., 1972), 4–19.

———. "Bibliographical Essay: An Appraisal of Latin American Slavery Through Literature," *Journal of Negro History*, 58, No. 4 (Oct., 1973).

———. "Martín Morúa Delgado," *Negro History Bulletin*, 36, No. 1 (Jan., 1973), 12.

———. "A Slave Poet in Latin America / Un poeta esclavo en América Latina," *Negro History Bulletin*, 37, No. 1 (1974), 198–199.

Davis, Toney, J. *Algunos poemas negros de Cuba y Ecuador*. Howard University M.A. Dissertation, May 1969.

DeCosta, Miriam. "The Evolution of the *Tema Negro* in Literature of the Spanish Baroque," *CLA Journal* (March, 1974).

———. "The Portrayal of Blacks in a Spanish Medieval Manuscript," *Negro History Bulletin*, 37, No. 1 (1974), 193–196.

Fernández de Castro, José A. "El aporte negro en las letras de Cuba en el Siglo XIX," *RBC*, 38 (1936), 46–66.

Harth, Dorothy Feldman. "La poesía afrocubana, sus raices e influencias," *Miscelánea de Estudios dedicados a Fernando Ortiz*. Havana, 1935.

Marquina, Rafael. "El negro en el teatro español antes de Lope de Vega," *Ultra*, 4, 555–568.

Monquió, Luis. "El negro en algunos poetas españoles americanos anteriores a 1800," *Estudios sobre literatura hispanoamericana y española*. Mexico, 1958.

Preto-Rodas, Richard A. "An Outline of Negritude as a Poetic Theme: Its Origins and Development," *Negritude as a Theme in the Poetry of the Portuguese-Speaking World*. University of Florida Press, 1970, v-13.

Sampson, Margaret. "Africa in Medieval Spanish Literature: Its Appearance in *El Caballero Cifar*," *Negro History Bulletin*, (Dec., 1969).

Valbuena Briones, Angel. "El tema negro en la poesía antillana," *Literatura hispanoamericana*. Barcelona: Gustavo Gili, 1963.

Valdés-Cruz, Rosa. "Tres poemas representativos de la poesía afroantillana," *Hispania*, (March, 1970), 39–45.

Wardropper, Bruce. "The Color Problem in Spanish Traditional Poetry," *Modern Language Notes* (May, 1960).

Weber de Kurlat, Frida. "El tipo del negro en el teatro de Lope de Vega: tradición y creación," *NRFH*, 19 (1970), 337–59.

MAJOR STUDIES

Alvarez Nazario, Manuel. *El elemento Afronegroide en el español de Puerto Rico*. Instituto de Cultura Puertorriqueña, 1961.

Amis, B. D. *The Negro in the Colombian Novel*. Ph.D. Dissertation. Ann Arbor, Michigan: University Microfilms, 1970.

Augier, Angel. *Nicolás Guillén: notas para un estudio biográfico-crítico (1938-1947)*. 2 vols. Havana, 1964.

Barreda, P. M. *La caracterización del protagonista negro en la novela cubana*. Ph.D. Dissertation. Ann Arbor, Michigan: University Microfilms, 1969.

Becco, Horacio Jorge. *Negros y morenos en el Cancionero Rioplatense*. Buenos Aires: Sociedad Argentina de Americanistas, 1953.

————. *El tema del negro en cantos, bailes y villancicos de los siglos XVI y XVII*. Buenos Aires, 1951.

Blanco, Tomás. *Sobre Palés Matos*. San Juan: Biblioteca de Autores Puertorriqueños, 1950.

Carruthers, Ben Frederic. *The Life, Work and Death of Plácido*. Ph.D. Dissertation. University of Illinois, 1941.

Cartey, Wilfred. *Black Images*. New York: Teachers College Press, 1970.

Coulthard, G. R. *Race and Colour in Caribbean Literature*. London, 1962.

Enguídanos, Miguel. *Poesía como vida: Luis Palés Matos*. Río Piedras, Puerto Rico: Editorial Universitaria, 1961.

Estupiñan Tello, Julio. *El negro en Esmeraldas*. Quito: Sr. Enrique Moncayo A. los Talleres Gráficos Quito, 1967.

Fernández de Castro, J. A. *Tema negro en la literatura cubana*. Havana, 1943.

Franco, José Luciano. *Afroámerica*. Havana, 1961.

————. *Folklore criollo y afrocubano*. Havana: Publicaciones de la Junta Nacional de Arqueología y Etnología, 1959.

Harth, Dorothy Feldman. *Nicolás Guillén and Afro-Cuban Poetry*. Columbia University M.A. Thesis. 1948.

Jahn, Janheinz. *Muntu (las culturas de la negritud)*. Madrid: Ediciones Guadarrama, 1970.

Johnson, Lemuel. *The Devil, the Gargoyle and the Buffoon: The Negro as Metaphor in Western Literature*. Port Washington, N.Y.: Kennikat Press, 1971.

Mansour, Monica. *La poesía negrista*. Mexico: Ediciones Era, 1973.

Martínez Estrada, Ezequial. *La poesía afrocubana de Nicolás Guillén*. Montevideo: Editorial Arca, 1966.

Pereda Valdés, Ildefonso. *Línea de color: ensayos afro-americanos*. Santiago: Ediciones Ercilla, 1938.

————. *El negro en la epopeya artiquista*. Montevideo: Barreiro y Ramos, 1964.

————. *El negro rioplatense y otros ensayos*. Montevideo: Claudio Garcia & Cia., 1937.

————. *Lo negro y lo mulato en la poesía cubana*. Montevideo: Corporacion Grafica, 1970.

Spratlin, Valaurez B. *Juan Latino, Slave and Humanist*. New York: Spinner Press, 1938.

Stimson, Frederick S. *Cuba's Romantic Poet: The Story of Plácido*. Chapel Hill: The University of North Carolina Press, 1964.

White, Florence E. *"Poesía negra" in the Works of Jorge de Lima, Nicolás Guillén and Jacques Roumain, 1927-1947*. Ph.D. Dissertation, University of Wisconsin, 1952.

The Contributors

Martha K. Cobb received the B.A. and M.A. degrees from Howard University, and a Ph.D. degree in Comparative Literature from Catholic University. An Associate Professor at Howard, she has published numerous articles on Afro-Hispanic literature in *Hispania, Black World, TESOL Quarterly*, the *CLA Journal*, the *Journal of Negro History* and the *Negro History Bulletin*.

Miriam DeCosta, the editor of this volume, is Chairman of the Department of Romance Languages at Howard University. She holds the B.A. degree in Spanish from Wellesley College, and the M.A. and Ph.D. degrees in Romance Languages from Johns Hopkins University. Her articles have appeared in the *CLA Journal, Black World, Modern Language Notes*, the *Negro History Bulletin* and other publications.

Constance Sparrow de García-Barrio is an honor graduate of West Chester State College. She received the M.A. degree from Temple University and the Ph.D. degree from the University of Pennsylvania, where she wrote a dissertation on the poetry of Nicolás Guillén.

Shirley Jackson, an Assistant Professor of Spanish at the District of Columbia Teachers College, initiated a course on the African influence in Hispanic literature. The former Ford Foundation Fellow received the B.A. degree from the University of Illinois and the M.A. from Southern Illinois University and is a doctoral candidate at George Washington University, where she is investigating the African presence in the contemporary Spanish American novel.

Howard M. Jason is Professor Emeritus and former Chairman of the Department of Modern Languages at Savannah State College. Before his retirement he also served as Chairman of the Humanities Division. He received the B.A. degree from Lincoln University in Pennsylvania, the M.A. degree from Columbia University and the Ph.D. degree from the Universidad Intramericana in Saltillo, Mexico.

Lemuel Johnson, who was born in Nigeria to Sierra Leonese parents, has published a critical study, *The Devil, the Gargoyle and the Buffoon: The Negro as Metaphor in Western Literature*, and is completing *Hottentots, Coolies and Messiahs: An Esthetic Foundation for African Expression*. *Highlife for Caliban* is his first collection of poems, and his short stories have appeared in numerous reviews and journals. He has taught at Fourah Bay College of the University of Sierra Leone and at Oberlin, and is presently an Associate Professor of English at the University of Michigan.

John F. Matheus, Professor Emeritus of Modern Foreign Languages at West Virginia State College, has had a distinguished career as a teacher and scholar. He was educated at Western Reserve University, Columbia University, the Sorbonne and the University of Chicago, and he is the author of more than fifty short stories, plays and articles.

Antonio Olliz Boyd is an Assistant Professor of Spanish and Portuguese at Temple University. He graduated magna cum laude from Long Island University and received the Masters degree from Georgetown University. His doctoral dissertation on *The Concept of Black Esthetics in Selected Works of Three Latin American Authors: Machado de Assis, Nicolás Guillén and Adalberto Ortiz*, was completed at Stanford University.

Adalberto Ortiz, the Afro-Ecuadorian novelist, poet and literary critic, is the author of novels such as *Juyungo* and *El espejo y la ventana*, for which he was awarded national prizes; of collections of short stories – *La entundada* and *La mala espada;* and of poetry – *Tierra, son y tambor, El animal herido* and *El vigilante insepulto*.

Valaurez B. Spratlin served as Professor and Chairman of the Department of Romance Languages of Howard University until his retirement and death in the Sixties. An outstanding teacher and scholar, he published a book, *Juan Latino, Slave and Humanist*, and many articles and reviews about Afro-Hispanic literature.

Leslie N. Wilson is an Associate Professor of Foreign Languages and Director of the Peace Corps Minority Intern Program at Florida A & M University. He received the B.A. degree from Temple University, the M.A. from the Universidad Nacional Autónoma de México and New York University and the Ph.D. summa cum laude from Inter-American University. He served as Zone Supervisor of English in Puerto Rico for ten years.

Carter G. Woodson, who served as Dean of the School of Liberal Arts at Howard University, founded the Association for the Study of Negro Life and History in 1915 and published the first issue of the *Journal of Negro History* in 1916. This distinguished teacher, historian and scholar was the author of more than thirty books, including *The Negro in Our History, The Education of the Negro Prior to 1861* and *Latin America in School and College Teaching Materials.*

Sylvia Wynter, born in Cuba of Jamaican parents, was educated at the universities of London (King's College) and Madrid. She has acted, danced, translated plays and published novels and plays, including *The Hills of Hebron* and *A Ballad for a Rebellion.* She has written numerous articles on Jamaican literature, Third World politics, and sixteenth-century Spain in her attempt to establish a conceptual critical framework outside of the European/North American world view.

Ann V. Young, an Assistant Professor of Spanish and French at Morgan State College, attended Morgan and the Universidad de Puerto Rico, from which she received the M.A. degree. She was awarded an NDEA grant to study in France and a fellowship from the Southern Fellowships Fund for study at the Johns Hopkins University, where she is a candidate for the Ph.D. degree in Romance Languages. A recent article, "'La Pena' as the Protagonist of García Lorca's *Romancero gitano,*" was published in the *CLA Journal.*

Index

Abu Bakr, 23
Abu Dulama Ibn Al Djaun, 23
Aguado, Pedro de, *The History of Venezuela*, 50
Aguado, Simón, 92, 124
Alarcón, Pedro Antonio, *El final de Norma*, 44
Alberti, Rafael, 103
Alfonso X, *Cántigas*, 5, 11-12, 14
Alix, Juan Antonio, 94
Allen, Alma C., "Literary Relations Between Spain and Africa," 29
Althusser, Louis, 15
Alvarez Gato, Juan, 31
Alvarez Nazario, Manuel, *El elemento afronegroide en el español de Puerto Rico*, 29
Amado, Jorge, *Jubiaba* and *Mar Morto*, 81
Amis, B. D., *The Negro in the Colombian Novel*, 72
Andrade, Roberto, 77
Antar Ibn Shaddad, 22-23
Apollinaire, Guillaume, 91
Arias Trujillo, Bernardo, *Rizaralda*, 81
Arozarena, Marcelino, 4, 63, 102, 116, 121, 142; *Canción negra sin color*, 119-120
Auerbach, Erich, *Mimesis*, 131
Auto de los Reyes Magos, 14, 29-30, 92

Ballagas, Emilio, 63, 98, 100-101, 102, 134, 137, 142
Baraka, Imamu, *Home*, 120
Barrionuevo, Jerónimo de, *Avisos*, 32
Baudet, Henri, *Paradise on Earth*, 12-13
Beleño C., Joaquín, 70, 73; *Gamboa Road Gang*, 70-71; *Curundú*, 71
Ben Said, 23
Bernardin de St. Pierre, Jacques-Henri, *Paul et Virginie*, 58
Blance, Eduardo, *Zárate*, 60; *Nannelote*, 60
Blanco, Andrés Eloy, 102
Blanco, Tomás, *Sobre Palés Matos*, 135
Bolívar, Rafael, "La negra," 60
Bontemps, Arna, 92
Bretón, Manuel, *La independencia*, 43
Brown Castillo, G., 105
Burton, Robert, *Anatomy of Melancholy*, 34

Caballero Cifar, El, 25
Cabello Balboa, M., 77
Cabral, Manuel de, 102
Cabrera, Lydia, 116
Calderón de la Barca, Pedro, 128; *Los hijos de la fortuna: Teágenes y Cariclea*, 33-35, 42; *El gran*

Williams, Chancellor, *The Destruction of Black Civilization*, 89
Woodson, Carter G., 3, 63
Wright, Richard, 4; *Native Son*, 81

Ximénez de Encisco, Diego, 25, 33, 39–40

Young, Karl, 14

Zapata Olivella, Manuel, 72
Ziriab, the "Black Nightingale," 23
Zoro, Fermín, *La sibila de los Andes*, 60